Collins Instant Revision

FRENCH GCSE Key Stage 4

Dave Carter
Series Editor: Jayne de Courcy

Collins Educational
An Imprint of HarperCollinsPublishers

Contents

D0586211

Published by Collins Educational
An imprint of HarperCollins*Publishers* Ltd
77–85 Fulham Palace Road
London W6 8JB

© HarperCollins*Publishers* Ltd 1999

First published 1999

ISBN 0 00 323514 9

British Library Cataloguing in Publication Data
A catalogue record for this publication is available from the British Library

Edited by Sue Chapple
Production by Anna Pauletti
Design by Gecko Limited
Cover design by Gecko Limited
Printed and bound in Italy by Eurografica

Acknowledgements

Illustrations
Gecko Ltd and John Plumb

Get the most out of your
Instant Revision cards

1 **Maximise your revision time.** You can carry the cards around with you anywhere. This means you can spend any spare moments looking at a card or two.

2 **Learn and remember what you need to know.** The cards contain all the really important things you need to know for your exam. All the information is set out clearly and concisely, making it easy for you to revise.

3 **Find out what you don't know.** The *Check yourself* cards and *Score* card help you see quickly and easily the topics you're good at and those you're not so good at.

The different sorts of cards

1 *Fact* cards – just what you need to know

Vocabulary and phrases
● There are cards for all the topics that you'll meet in your GCSE French exam. The more difficult phrases are on the reverse side of the cards; you only need to learn these if you are sitting the Higher Tier exam.

Grammar
● All the important grammatical structures are covered, set out in a way that makes them easy to revise and remember.

Listening, Speaking, Reading and Writing skills
● Look at these cards just before you go into each of the exams.

2 *Check yourself* cards – find out how much you know and boost your grade

● Each *Check yourself* card is linked to a *Fact* card or cards.

● The questions are quick to answer. They aren't actual exam questions but they will show you what you do and don't know.

● The back of each *Check yourself* card gives you the answers **plus** tutorial help and guidance to boost your exam grade.

● There are points for each question. The total number of points for all the questions on a card is always 20. When you check your answers, fill in the score box alongside each answer with the number of points you feel you scored.

3 The *Score* card – an instant picture of your strengths and weaknesses

● The front of the *Score* card lists all the *Check yourself* cards.

● As you complete each *Check yourself* card, record your points on the *Score* card. This will show you instantly which areas you need to spend more time revising.

● The graph on the back of the *Score* card lets you plot your points against GCSE grades. This will give you a rough idea of how you are doing in each area. Of course, this is only a rough idea because the questions aren't real exam questions!

Use these Instant Revision cards on your own – or revise with a friend or relative. See who can get the highest score!

L'ÉCOLE

Mon école est assez grande.	My school is quite large.
Il y a environ mille élèves et soixante profs.	There are about 1,000 pupils and 60 teachers.
C'est une école mixte.	It's a mixed school.
En été on a cinq semaines de vacances.	In summer we have five weeks holiday.
Je vais à l'école du lundi au vendredi.	I go to school from Monday to Friday.
Je n'ai pas cours le samedi.	I don't have lessons on Saturday.
Les cours commencent à neuf heures moins le quart.	Lessons begin at quarter to nine.
L'école finit à quatre heures.	School ends at four o'clock.
Nous avons cinq cours par jour.	We have five lessons a day.
J'ai beaucoup de devoirs.	I have a lot of homework.
Le collège n'est pas loin de ma maison.	School is not far from my house.
Je viens au collège à pied.	I walk to school.
Je rentre à la maison pour déjeuner.	I go home for lunch.
Je dois porter un uniforme.	I have to wear a uniform.
Je porte une chemise blanche et une cravate bleue.	I wear a white shirt and a blue tie.
Les filles portent une jupe grise.	The girls wear a grey skirt.
Je suis en seconde.	I'm in Year 11.
Mon frère est en sixième.	My brother is in Year 7.
J'ai une sœur à l'école primaire.	I have a sister at primary school.
Mes matières préférées sont les maths et l'histoire.	My favourite subjects are maths and history.
Je déteste les sciences.	I hate science.
Mon professeur de chimie s'appelle Mme Martin.	My chemistry teacher is called Mrs Martin.
Je n'aime pas les profs.	I don't like the teachers.
Je suis bon(ne) élève.	I am a good student.
J'ai de mauvaises notes en géographie.	I get bad marks in geography.
Je suis bon(ne)/nul(le) en EPS/anglais.	I'm good/hopeless at games/English.
L'espagnol est difficile.	Spanish is hard.

1

This topic lends itself easily to lots of personal opinions:

Je trouve l'histoire très intéressante.	I find history very interesting.
Mais les maths, c'est vraiment ennuyeux, et je suis nul(le).	But maths is really boring, and I'm useless.
J'aime bien l'école – les profs sont sympas, et j'y vois tous mes copains/toutes mes copines.	I really like school – the teachers are nice, and I see all my friends there.
Je ne supporte pas le collège – les profs me donnent trop de travail, et mes parents me critiquent toujours.	I really can't stand school – the teachers give me too much work, and my parents are always criticising me.

You can also make references to the future:

Cette année je vais passer des examens importants.	This year I'm going to take some important exams.
L'année prochaine j'espère retourner au collège pour continuer mes études.	Next year I hope to come back to school to continue my education.
Je vais étudier les langues et le commerce, car je voudrais travailler à l'étranger.	I'm going to study languages and business studies, as I'd like to work abroad.

and to the past:

L'année passée je n'ai pas travaillé, mais maintenant je fais des progrès.	Last year I didn't work, but now I'm making progress.

Even when the verb is in the present tense, you can move up to Higher Level performance by adding extra details:

Je travaille beaucoup – tous les soirs et le week-end aussi.	I work hard – every evening and the weekend too.
Pour réussir dans la vie, il faut bien travailler à l'école, pour avoir des qualifications.	To succeed in life, you have to work hard at school to get qualifications.

or by giving reasons:

J'étudie les maths parce que je trouve ça facile, et je suis assez bon(ne).	I study maths because I find it easy, and I am quite good.
J'ai choisi l'anglais à cause de mon père, qui est prof de langues.	I chose English because of my father, who is a languages teacher.

Check yourself 1

L'école

A. Ecrivez en français:

1 (1)

2 (1)

3 20/20 Excellent (1)

When you are speaking or writing about visuals, there is often more than one possible answer. As long as your answer fits the visual, you will get the credit for it.

B. Answer in French:

4 Les cours commencent à quelle heure? (1)

5 Où est-ce que tu manges à midi? (1)

6 Le collège est à quelle distance de chez toi? (1)

C. Say in French:

7 I hate French because it's boring. (2)

8 I've been learning German for three years. (2)

9 Next year I'm going to study languages and history. (2)

It's better to try to answer in sentences – you'll learn more than if you simply use a short phrase.

D. Say in French:

10 After school I hope to go to university to continue my education. (2)

11 I like geography because of the teacher, who is very amusing. (2)

12 I would like to be a doctor, but I'm not very good at science. (2)

13 I like all lessons, apart from sport – I'm hopeless. (2)

Sentences containing *pour* (+ infinitive), *qui*, *mais*, *sauf* (or *à part*) will really get you up to Higher Level.

A

1 J'aime/J'adore l'informatique. (1)

2 Je déteste/Je n'aime pas l'EPS/le sport. (1)

3 Je suis bon(ne) en sciences. *OR*
J'ai de bonnes notes en sciences. (1)

B

4 Les cours commencent à neuf heures moins le quart. (1) Any
sensible time will of course be accepted, so if you're not sure
how to say 'quarter to nine', stick to *neuf heures* (nine o'clock).

5 A midi, je mange à la cantine/au collège/à la maison. (1)
Again, there are a number of likely answers; choose the one
you are most comfortable with.

6 Le collège est à deux kilomètres de chez moi. (or any
reasonable distance) (1) Remember to use *à* before the
distance. You could equally well say *de ma maison*, but it is
probably easier to use the same form as in the question.

C

7 Je déteste le français (1) parce que c'est ennuyeux. (1)

8 J'apprends l'allemand (1) depuis trois ans. (1) Remember to
use the present tense after *depuis* (I have been learning).

9 L'année prochaine je vais étudier (1) les langues et l'histoire. (1)
Don't forget, school subjects have an article in front.

D Any error in **either** underlined section means maximum 1 mark.

10 Après le collège, j'espère <u>aller à l'université</u> <u>pour continuer
mes études</u>. (2) Note the two infinitives: *aller* as the second
of a pair of verbs, and *continuer* because it follows *pour*.

11 J'aime la géographie <u>à cause du professeur</u>, <u>qui est très
amusant</u>. (2) You can only use *parce que* before a clause which
contains a verb.

12 <u>Je voudrais être médecin</u>, mais je ne suis pas <u>très bon(ne) en
sciences</u>. (2) Use *en* after *bon* or *doué* (both mean 'good at').

13 J'aime <u>tous les cours à part le sport</u> – je suis nul(le). (2)
Note *nul* (masc), *nulle* (fem).

TOTAL

J'habite une grande maison.	I live in a big house.
Tu habites une maison ou un appartement?	Do you live in a house or a flat?
Mon frère habite un village à la campagne.	My brother lives in a village in the country.
Mon adresse est cinquante-trois rue de la Poste.	My address is 53 Post Office Street.
J'habite près/loin du collège.	I live near/a long way from school.
Le collège est à cinq minutes.	School is five minutes away.
Il y a un jardin devant la maison.	There is a garden in front of the house.
La maison est assez vieille.	The house is quite old.
C'est une maison à trois étages.	It's a three-storey house.
Il y a trois chambres, un salon et une salle à manger.	There are three bedrooms, a living-room and a dining-room.
Ma sœur a sa propre chambre.	My sister has her own bedroom.
Ma chambre est bleue et blanche.	My bedroom is blue and white.
J'ai un lit et une armoire.	I have a bed and a wardrobe.
Je fais mon lit/la vaisselle.	I make my bed/do the washing-up.
J'aide ma mère à la maison.	I help my mother in the house.
Mon frère range la chambre.	My brother tidies the bedroom.
On prend le petit déjeuner à quelle heure?	What time do we have breakfast?
Tu voudrais téléphoner chez toi?	Would you like to phone home?
La machine à laver ne marche pas.	The washing machine isn't working.
Je n'ai pas de serviette.	I haven't got a towel.
J'ai besoin de savon.	I need some soap.
Tu as une brosse à dents?	Have you got a toothbrush?
J'ai oublié mon shampooing.	I've forgotten my shampoo.
Voici ta chambre.	Here is your bedroom.
La salle de bains est juste en face.	The bathroom is just opposite.
Je me couche d'habitude à onze heures.	I usually go to bed at 11 o'clock.
Tu as vu le match à la télé?	Did you see the match on TV?
Je regarde souvent les feuilletons.	I often watch soaps.
Qu'est-ce qu'il y a à la télévision?	What's on television?
Mon émission préférée, c'est ...	My favourite programme is ...
Je n'écoute pas la radio.	I don't listen to the radio.

Nous habitons à deux kilomètres du centre-ville.

We live two kilometres from the town centre.

L'école est à vingt minutes de chez moi.

School is a 20 minute walk from home.

J'aime bien ma chambre. Elle est très jolie.

I love my room. It's very pretty.

Les murs sont blancs, et les rideaux sont verts.

The walls are white and the curtains are green.

Tu habites loin du centre-ville?

Do you live far from the town centre?

Ma sœur vient d'acheter un appartement neuf.

My sister has just bought a brand new flat.

Je partage ma chambre avec mon frère.

I share my room with my brother.

Mes soeurs aussi partagent leur chambre – elles détestent ça!

My sisters share a bedroom too – they hate it.

Dans ma chambre, j'ai une table pour faire mes devoirs.

In my bedroom, I have a table to do my homework on.

Je n'ai pas de télévision dans ma chambre – mes parents ne sont pas d'accord.

I don't have a television in my bedroom – my parents won't agree.

Nous aidons nos parents à la maison.

We help our parents in the house.

Moi, je passe l'aspirateur, et mon frère fait le jardinage.

I do the vacuuming, and my brother does the gardening.

Nous faisons tous la vaisselle.

We all do the washing up.

Tu peux regarder la télé si tu veux – ça ne me gêne pas du tout.

You can watch TV if you like – it doesn't bother me at all.

Je regarde les infos à la télé, mais dans le journal, je ne regarde que les pages de sport.

I watch the news on TV, but in the paper, I only read the sports pages.

J'adore les émissions sur les animaux sauvages – je les trouve très intéressantes.

I love programmes on wild animals – I find them very interesting.

Je ne lis jamais de magazines, car ils sont bêtes, et en plus ils sont très chers.

I never read magazines, because they are stupid, and also they are very expensive.

J'aime bien lire – surtout des romans policiers.

I love reading – especially detective novels.

Check yourself

A la maison/les média

A Que fais-tu pour aider à la maison?

1   2   3

(1)   (1)   (1)

B Answer in French:

4 Il y a combien de chambres chez toi? (1)

5 Tu habites une petite maison? (1)

6 Le collège est loin de chez toi? (1)

Remember, you will get little credit for *Oui/Non* answers. It's much better to use a full sentence, and more useful revision too. Remember also that this sort of question doesn't have a right or wrong answer – there may be several appropriate answers.

C Say in French:

7 My room is very nice, but it is too small. (2)

8 I don't like watching sport on television. (2)

9 I love documentaries on animals. (2)

D Say in French:

10 My brother never helps in the house, because he has too much homework. (2)

11 Can I watch television? Does it bother you? (2)

12 I wouldn't like to share a bedroom, especially not with my little brother. (2)

13 Can I help you? I could do the washing-up? (2)

A

1 Je fais la vaisselle. (1)

2 Je passe l'aspirateur. (1)

3 Je fais mon lit. (1)

B

4 Il y a deux/trois/quatre/cinq chambres. (1)

5 Oui, j'habite une petite maison/ma maison est petite. *OR*
Non, j'habite une grande maison/ma maison est grande. (1)
You could also say simply *Non, elle est grande.*

6 Oui, le collège est à cinq kilomètres/vingt-cinq minutes de
chez moi. *OR*
Non, le collège est à deux minutes/deux cents mètres de
chez moi. (1) You could also say *Oui, c'est très loin* or *Non, c'est
tout près* – as long as you avoid a straight *Oui* or *Non.*

C

7 <u>Ma</u> chambre est très <u>belle/jolie</u>, (1) mais <u>elle</u> est trop <u>petite</u>. (1)
Notice all the words (underlined) which follow from *chambre*
being feminine.

8 Je n'aime pas regarder le sport (1) à la télévision. (1)
On TV = *à la télévision.*

9 J'adore les documentaires (1) sur les animaux. (1)
But here 'on' = *sur.*

D Any error in **either** underlined section means maximum 1 mark.

10 Mon frère <u>n'aide jamais</u> à la maison, parce qu'il a <u>trop de
devoirs</u>. (2) Like *beaucoup*, *trop* before a noun is always
followed by *de.*

11 <u>Je peux regarder</u> la télévision? <u>Ça vous gêne?</u> (2)
Asking permission politely is an important skill to learn.

12 <u>Je ne voudrais pas partager</u> une chambre, <u>surtout pas</u> avec
mon petit frère. (2) When it is not with a verb, *pas* is often
used without *ne.*

13 <u>Je peux vous aider? Je pourrais faire</u> la vaisselle? (2)
Offering to do something is another important skill. Using
the conditional of *pouvoir* is one way of doing this.

TOTAL

LA SANTÉ, LA FORME ET LA NOURRITURE

J'ai mal au bras.	My arm hurts.
Où est-ce que ça fait mal?	Where does it hurt?
J'ai mal aux dents.	I have toothache.
Je me suis cassé la jambe.	I have broken my leg.
Elle s'est fait mal au genou.	She has hurt her knee.
Je suis enrhumé(e).	I've got a cold.
Il faut aller chez le dentiste/chez le médecin/à l'hôpital.	You must go to the dentist's/to the doctor's/to hospital.
Au secours!	Help!
Je voudrais un rendez-vous avec le médecin.	I'd like an appointment with the doctor.
J'adore le chocolat.	I love chocolate.
Je déteste les carottes.	I hate carrots.
Je suis allergique au poisson.	I'm allergic to fish.
Je n'aime pas beaucoup le fromage.	I don't like cheese very much.
Voulez-vous me passer les pommes de terre/le sel, s'il vous plaît?	Will you pass me the potatoes/salt, please?
Je n'ai pas de couteau.	I haven't got a knife.
Vous avez une table pour deux personnes?	Do you have a table for two?
Monsieur/Madame/Mademoiselle, je voudrais voir la carte, s'il vous plaît.	Waiter, I'd like to see the menu, please.
Je prends le menu à quatre-vingts francs.	I'll have the 80 franc menu.
Qu'est-ce que c'est, le plat du jour?	What is the dish of the day?
Pour commencer, je voudrais le potage.	To start, I'll have the soup.
Puis je prendrai un steak-frites.	Then I'll have steak and chips.
Je prendrai un peu de fromage.	I'll have a little cheese.
Je ne veux pas de dessert.	I don't want any pudding.
Le service est compris?	Is the service charge included?
Où sont les toilettes/les téléphones?	Where are the toilets/telephones?
L'addition, s'il vous plaît.	Can I have the bill, please?
Qu'est-ce que vous avez comme glaces/sandwichs?	What sort of ice-creams/sandwiches have you got?

Je suis tombé(e) en jouant
au football.

Moi je trouve que le sport est
dangereux – on peut se faire mal.

Je suis très enrhumé(e), alors je
tousse et j'ai mal à la tête.

Hier j'ai travaillé dans le jardin, et
maintenant j'ai mal au dos.

Pouvez-vous me donner quelque
chose pour mon rhume?

Portez cette ordonnance à
la pharmacie.

Prenez deux comprimés trois fois
par jour, avant les repas.

C'est quoi, exactement, le
bœuf bourguignon?

Tu en veux encore?

Oui, je veux bien, c'est délicieux.

Non, merci. Ça suffit.

Le dîner est servi à partir de
quelle heure?

Vous avez une table près de
la fenêtre?

Vous préférez manger à la terrasse,
ou à l'intérieur?

Ma viande est froide/trop cuite/
n'est pas assez cuite.

Il y a une erreur dans l'addition.

Nous n'avons pas pris de vin.

Le service était très lent – j'ai
attendu une demi-heure.

Manger trop de matières grasses/
de choses sucrées est mauvais
pour la santé.

Vous devez manger des fruits,
des légumes et des céréales.

Il est aussi important de faire
du sport.

I fell while playing football.

I think that sport is dangerous
– you can hurt yourself.

I have a bad cold, so I've got a
cough and a headache.

Yesterday I worked in the garden,
and now I have backache.

Can you give me something for
my cold?

Take this prescription to
the chemist's.

Take two tablets three times a
day, before meals.

What exactly is beef burgundy?

Would you like some more?

Yes, I'd love some, it's delicious.

No thank you, I've had enough.

What time do you start
serving dinner?

Do you have a table near
the window?

Would you rather eat on the
terrace, or indoors?

My steak is cold/over-cooked/
not well enough cooked.

There is a mistake in the bill.

We didn't have any wine.

The service was very slow –
I waited half an hour.

Eating too much fat/too many
sweet things is bad for your
health.

You ought to eat fruit,
vegetables and cereals.

It is also important to do
some sport.

La santé, la forme et la nourriture

A   Où est-ce que ça fait mal?

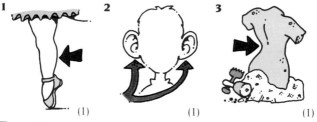

1   2   3

(1)   (1)   (1)

B   Say in French:

4   I'd like a table for four, please. (1)

5   I haven't got a spoon. (1)

6   For pudding, I'd like an ice-cream. (1)

C   Ask in French:

7   ... if you should take the pills before or after meals. (2)

8   ... if the chemist has anything for sore throats. (2)

9   ... if your penfriend has a headache or a temperature. (2)

D   At the restaurant:

10   Say you didn't order chicken, you ordered ham. (2)

11   Tell the waiter you asked for a bottle of wine ten minutes ago. (2)

12   Explain that your friend is a vegetarian, and ask if he can have an omelette. (2)

13   Ask what desserts are available, as you are allergic to nuts. (2)

Be careful when using your dictionary. If you look up a verb, make sure you use the right part. If you look up 'ago', or 'vegetarian', you need to check the examples. If you look up 'nuts' make sure you choose the right sort!

A

1 J'ai mal à la jambe. (1)

2 J'ai mal aux oreilles. (1)

3 J'ai mal au dos. (1) It is important to remember whether the part of the body is masculine, feminine or plural.

B

4 Je voudrais une table pour quatre personnes, s'il vous plaît. (1)

5 Je n'ai pas de cuiller. (1)

6 Comme dessert, je voudrais une glace. (1)

C It is important to be able to ask questions. It usually doesn't matter whether you use tone of voice (No 7), inversion (No 8) or *Est-ce que* (No 9).

7 Je dois prendre les comprimés (1) avant ou après les repas? (1)

8 Avez-vous quelque chose (1) pour le mal de gorge? (1)
If you couldn't figure out how to say the second half of this, you could always say: *J'ai mal à la gorge. Pouvez-vous me donner quelque chose?*

9 Est-ce que tu as mal à la tête, (1) ou de la fièvre? (1)
Be careful when you look up a word in the dictionary – the word *température* is not the best one here.

D Any error in **either** underlined section means maximum 1 mark.

10 <u>Je n'ai pas commandé</u> le poulet, <u>j'ai commandé</u> le jambon. (2)
In the dictionary, you will find the infinitive *commander*, but here you need the past participle. Note the definite article with the food.

11 <u>J'ai demandé</u> une bouteille de vin <u>il y a dix minutes</u>. (2)
The examples in the dictionary will indicate that *il y a* comes before the time.

12 <u>Mon ami est végétarien;</u> <u>est-ce qu'il peut avoir</u> une omelette? (2)

13 <u>Qu'est-ce que vous avez</u> comme dessert, car je suis <u>allergique aux noix</u>? (2)

Il s'appelle Paul.	His name is Paul.
J'ai quinze ans.	I am 15.
Son anniversaire est le dix-sept mars.	Her birthday is the 17th of March.
Elles sont italiennes.	They are Italian.
Elle est fille unique.	She is an only daughter.
Je suis fils unique.	I am an only son.
Elle a deux frères.	She has two brothers.
Ma sœur est plus jeune que mon frère.	My sister is younger than my brother.
Mon frère est célibataire.	My brother isn't married.
Ça s'écrit G-U-I-L-L-A-U-M-E.	It's spelt G-U-I-L-L-A-U-M-E.
Ma mère est plus âgée que mon père.	My mother is older than my father.
Mes parents sont divorcés.	My parents are divorced.
J'ai deux frères jumeaux.	I have two twin brothers.
Elle a deux sœurs jumelles.	She has two twin sisters.
Il y a quatre personnes dans ma famille.	There are four people in my family.
Il n'habite pas chez ses parents.	He doesn't live with his parents.
Elle a les cheveux frisés.	She has curly hair.
Il a les yeux verts.	He has green eyes.
Je suis assez grand(e).	I am quite tall.
Mon cousin est égoïste.	My cousin is selfish.
Mon oncle est très gentil.	My uncle is very nice.
Ma tante est sympa.	My aunt is nice.
Ma demi-sœur est méchante.	My half sister is nasty.
Je m'entends bien avec ma belle-mère.	I get on well with my step-mother.
Je ne m'entends pas avec mon frère.	I don't get on with my brother.
Il m'énerve.	He gets on my nerves.
Elle est très sportive.	She is very sporting.
Il n'est pas amusant.	He is not much fun.
J'ai une souris qui s'appelle Max.	I have a mouse called Max.
Nous avons beaucoup d'animaux à la maison.	We have lots of animals at home.

To produce Higher Level work on this topic, you need to be sure to go beyond the language you learned in Year 8. There are a number of ways you can do this.

● Add an extra detail to your basic statement. This might be a reason, an explanation, an example, or simply an extra piece of information:

Je m'entends très bien avec ma mère. Elle écoute toujours mes problèmes.

I get on very well with my mother. She always listens to my problems.

J'aime bien mon père, mais quelquefois il est trop strict.

I love my father, but sometimes he is too strict.

Mon petit frère est vraiment bête, et il fait trop de bruit.

My little brother is really silly, and he makes too much noise.

Mon meilleur copain s'appelle Luc. Je peux lui parler de tout.

My best friend is called Luc. I can talk to him about anything.

Je préfère être avec mes amis, car ils ont le même âge et les mêmes goûts que moi.

I prefer being with my friends, as they are the same age and have the same tastes as me.

J'ai beaucoup de cousins et de cousines, et j'ai aussi un neveu.

I have lots of cousins, and I also have a nephew.

● As well as stating facts, make sure you express personal opinions:

Je dois toujours rester à la maison avec ma petite sœur. Ce n'est pas juste.

I always have to stay at home with my little sister. It's not fair.

Je ne peux jamais sortir pendant la semaine. J'en ai marre.

I can never go out during the week. I'm fed up with it.

J'aime bien être fille unique. Mes parents s'occupent de moi tout le temps.

I love being an only child. I have my parents' attention all the time.

J'adore avoir une grande famille. On ne se sent jamais seul.

I love having a large family. You never feel alone.

Ma sœur ne range jamais ses affaires. Ça m'énerve!

My sister never puts her things away. It drives me mad.

Je ne m'entends pas avec mon frère aîné. Il est très égoïste.

I don't get on with my older brother. He's very selfish.

Moi, ma famille et mes amis

Complete these descriptions:

1 Ma sœur ...

(1)

2 Mon père ...

(1)

3 Ma grand-mère ...

(1)

Say in French:

4 My sister is nice. (1)

5 She has a dog called Prince. (1)

6 My brother is younger than me. (1)

The following people are talking about their families. How do they get on together? (Well? OK? Badly?)

7 Je me dispute quelquefois avec mes parents, mais la plupart du temps, ça va. (2)

8 J'aime bien mes parents, mais ils me critiquent toujours. Ma sœur, par contre, fait tout ce qu'elle veut – elle ne se plaint pas! (2)

9 On ne dirait pas, car mes parents sont divorcés, et mon frère n'habite plus avec nous, mais ils sont comme mes meilleurs amis. (2)

In this kind of exercise, you are not trying to pick out details, but to reach a general conclusion. For example, a really strong negative might be more important than two minor positives.

Say in French:

10 I can only go out on Friday night and Saturday. (2)

11 I am the same age as my cousin, but we don't have the same tastes. (2)

12 I love my brothers, but sometimes they get on my nerves. (2)

13 If I have a problem, I would rather talk to my friends. (2)

A

1 (Ma sœur) porte des lunettes. (1)

2 (Mon père) a les cheveux courts. (1)

3 (Ma grand-mère) a quatre-vingt-treize ans. (1)

B

4 Ma sœur est sympa/gentille. (1) Note that *sympa* does not change in the feminine, but *gentil* adds *le*.

5 Elle a un chien qui s'appelle Prince. (1)
The *qui* is important here.

6 Mon frère est plus jeune que moi. (1) Notice the use of *moi* (not *me* or *je*) after *que*. Also with prepositions like *avant*, *avec*.

C Although the answers to these questions are in themselves straightforward, the overall understanding required means your Higher Level reading skills are being tested.

7 OK. (2) The phrase *ça va* with *la plupart du temps* (most of the time) means that the relationship is generally positive, but *ça va* is not very enthusiastic.

8 Badly. (2) The main impression is of ill-feeling and jealousy, despite the *J'aime bien mes parents*.

9 Well. (2) In spite of the negatives, the phrase *meilleurs amis* clearly indicates a very positive relationship.

D Any error in **either** underlined section means maximum 1 mark.

10 <u>Je peux sortir seulement</u> <u>le vendredi soir et le samedi</u>. (2)
Equally good for the first half would be *Je ne peux sortir que*.
Remember to use *le* before days of the week to indicate regular events.

11 <u>J'ai le même âge que</u> mon cousin, mais nous n'avons pas <u>les mêmes goûts</u>. (2) Note the use of *que* after *même* (the same as).

12 <u>J'aime bien</u> mes frères, mais <u>quelquefois ils m'énervent</u>. (2) Words like *quelquefois* never come between the subject and the verb. For the second half of the sentence, you could say *quelquefois ils sont casse-pieds*.

13 <u>Si j'ai un problème</u>, je préfère en <u>parler à mes copains/copines</u>. (2) A phrase using *si* (if) always shows Higher Level skills.

LE TEMPS LIBRE, LES LOISIRS, LES VACANCES ET LES FETES

Mon sport préféré, c'est la natation.	My favourite sport is swimming.
La lecture ne m'intéresse pas.	I'm not interested in reading.
Je collectionne les disques/CD.	I collect records/CDs.
J'aime la danse.	I like dance/dancing.
Je suis fou/folle de cinéma.	I'm mad about the cinema.
Je déteste le jardinage.	I hate gardening.
Mon frère adore les sports d'hiver.	My brother loves winter sports.
L'année dernière, nous sommes allés en Suisse.	Last year we went to Switzerland.
Je vais passer Noël chez mon père.	I'm going to spend Christmas with my father.
Tu veux aller au bord de la mer cette année?	Do you want to go to the sea-side this year?
Je préfère aller à l'étranger.	I prefer to go abroad.
Ce soir, on va au complexe sportif.	Tonight we'll go to the sports centre.
Il est ouvert de neuf heures à vingt-deux heures.	It's open from 9 a.m. till 10 p.m.
Marie veut aller à la piscine.	Marie wants to go to the swimming pool.
Luc préfère jouer au badminton.	Luc prefers to play badminton.
J'aime sortir le soir.	I like going out in the evening.
Si on allait à la discothèque?	How about going to the discotheque?
Jeudi soir, on va au club de jeunes.	On Thursday night, we go to the youth club.
Ça coûte cher?	Is it expensive?
Non, ça coûte quinze francs seulement.	No, it only costs 15 francs.
Dimanche, il y a une fête au village.	On Sunday there is a festival in the village.
Il y a un bal et une petite foire.	There's a dance, and a small fair.
Tu veux aller au cirque?	Do you want to go to the circus?
Non merci, c'est cruel.	No thank you, they're cruel.
Oui, tu as raison.	Yes, you are right.
Non, je ne suis pas d'accord.	No, I don't agree.
Tu as beaucoup d'argent de poche?	Do you get a lot of pocket money?
Mes parents me donnent cent francs par semaine.	My parents give me 100 francs a week.

17

This is an ideal topic for referring to past, present and future events. When talking about leisure activities, it's quite easy to say what you usually do (e.g. *le vendredi soir* – on Friday night), what you did last week (*la semaine dernière*), and what you are going to do next weekend (*le week-end prochain*). For holidays, again you can talk about where you usually go, where you went last year (*l'année dernière*), and where you are going this year (*cette année*).

La semaine prochaine, mon père va m'emmener à un match de foot.	Next week, my father is going to take me to a football match.
Hier soir je suis allé(e) au cinéma avec mes copains.	Last night I went to the cinema with my friends.
Normalement, le dimanche je vais chez mes grands-parents à la campagne.	Normally, on Sunday I go to visit my grandparents in the country.
L'hiver dernier, je suis allé(e) en Italie, où j'ai fait du ski.	Last winter, I went to Italy, where I went ski-ing.
L'année prochaine, pendant les grandes vacances, j'espère aller aux Etats-Unis avec mes parents.	Next year, during the summer holidays, I hope to go to the United States with my parents.
En été, nous allons toujours au même endroit. C'est un petit village au pays de Galles.	In summer, we always go to the same place. It's a little village in Wales.

For holidays you can also expand on the bare facts by giving extra detail about activities, the weather, excursions, etc. Don't forget to give some opinions.

Il a fait très chaud, alors on a mangé dehors tous les soirs.	It was very warm, so we ate outside every evening.
S'il fait beau, nous jouons sur la plage, et s'il pleut, nous allons en ville pour faire du shopping.	If the weather is good, we play on the beach, and if it rains, we go into town to do some shopping.
Un jour, nous avons visité la vieille ville de Carcassonne. C'était très intéressant.	One day we visited the old town of Carcassonne. It was very interesting.
S'il faisait assez beau, je passerais mes vacances en Angleterre.	If the weather was good enough, I would spend my holidays in England.
Je ne reçois pas assez d'argent pour acheter beaucoup de vêtements.	I don't get enough money to buy many clothes.

Le temps libre, les loisirs, les vacances et les fêtes

A **Answer in French:** (It is more useful for revision purposes to give a full sentence.)

1 Quel est ton sport préféré?

2 Où as-tu passé les vacances?

3 Quel est ton passe-temps favori?

(1)   (1)   (1)

B **Match the two halves of the sentences:**

4 J'adore les vacances ...   **a)** je préfère faire du sport. (1)

5 Je n'aime pas lire, ...   **b)** écouter mes CD. (1)

6 Dans ma chambre, j'aime ...   **c)** au bord de la mer. (1)

C **Say in French:**

7 I don't get much pocket money. (2)

8 I'm going to spend two weeks in the mountains. (2)

9 Last week my uncle took me to a basketball match. (2)

D **Say in French:**

10 I have never been on holiday with my friends. (2)

11 My parents don't give me enough pocket money. (2)

12 If I had the time, I would spend a month in Wales. (2)

13 I had an awful holiday in Spain. It rained every day. (2)

A

1 Mon sport préféré est la natation. (1) Remember that *ton* in the question becomes *mon* in the answer.

2 J'ai passé les vacances au bord de la mer. (1) Note that *vacances* is plural.

3 J'aime collectionner les timbres. (1) You don't have to repeat the question when you answer it, but of course you could say *Mon passe-temps préféré, c'est collectionner les timbres*.

B

4c (1)   **5a** (1)   **6b** (1)

Look at all the questions before you commit yourself. Here, for example, 5c (*Je n'aime pas lire au bord de la mer*) just about works, but leaves you with no possibility for No 4.

C

7 Je ne reçois pas (1) beaucoup d'argent de poche. (1) After *beaucoup* you should always use *de/d'*.

8 Je vais passer deux semaines (1) à la montagne. (1) Note the use of *passer* meaning 'to spend time': *j'ai passé* (past); *je vais passer* (future).

9 La semaine dernière mon oncle (1) m'a emmené(e) à un match de basket. (1) Note the position of *me* before the verb – and therefore it becomes *m'* before a vowel.

D Any error in **either** underlined section means maximum 1 mark.

10 <u>Je ne suis jamais allé(e)</u> en vacances <u>avec mes copains</u>. (2) Note the position of *jamais* in the perfect tense. You could use *amis* instead of *copains* (or *amies/copines* if you wanted to make it clear they were all girls).

11 Mes parents <u>ne me donnent pas</u> <u>assez d'argent</u> de poche. (2) It's easy to forget to make the verb plural by adding *...ent*. To say 'enough' you always need *assez de/d'* in French.

12 <u>Si j'avais le temps</u>, je passerais un mois au pays de Galles. (2) You often need the imperfect tense after *si*, followed by another phrase in which the verb is in the conditional.

13 J'ai passé <u>des vacances affreuses</u> en Espagne. <u>Il a plu</u> tous les jours. (2) Even when the English would say 'a holiday', *vacances* is plural in French. Note the use of the perfect tense for the weather.

Voici mon frère, Paul.	This is my brother, Paul.
Je vous présente Mme Lafayette.	May I introduce Mme Lafayette.
Enchanté(e).	Pleased to meet you.
Salut!	Hi!/Cheerio!
Bonjour.	Hello/Good day/Good morning.
Bonsoir.	Good evening.
Bonne nuit.	Good night.
Bonne journée.	Have a nice day.
Au revoir.	Goodbye.
A bientôt.	See you soon.
A demain.	See you tomorrow.
Félicitations.	Congratulations.
Tu veux aller au concert avec moi?	Do you want to go to the concert with me?
Si on allait au bar?	How about going to the bar?
Ça te dit d'aller au cinéma?	Do you fancy going to the cinema?
Oui, je veux bien.	Yes I'd love to.
Ce serait super.	That would be great.
Non merci, je ne peux pas.	No thanks, I can't.
Je regrette, j'ai du travail à faire.	I'm sorry, I have some work to do.
Je dois sortir avec mes parents.	I have to go out with my parents.
Qu'est-ce qu'il y a à faire ici?	What is there to do here?
Qu'est-ce qu'il y a au cinéma?	What's on at the cinema?
C'est un film d'épouvante.	It's a horror film.
Qu'est-ce que tu aimes comme films?	What sort of films do you like?
C'est quoi comme concert?	What sort of concert is it?
Le match commence/finit à quelle heure?	What time does the match start/finish?
Je voudrais trois places.	I'd like three seats.
Tu as aimé le film?	Did you like the film?
Oui, c'était très bien/excellent.	Yes, it was very good/excellent.
Non, c'était ennuyeux/nul.	No it was boring/rubbish.
On se rencontre devant la gare.	Let's meet outside the station.
Rendez-vous à huit heures et demie.	Let's meet at half past eight.
Si on se voyait au bar?	How about meeting at the café?

On pourrait aller au concert si tu veux.	We could go to the concert if you like.
Tu veux venir avec moi au cinéma?	Do you want to come to the cinema with me?
Tu voudrais m'accompagner à la boum?	Would you like to go to the party with me?
Ecoute, ce soir il y a un concert en ville. On y va?	Listen, there's a concert in town tonight. Shall we go?
Je peux inviter un(e) ami(e)?	Can I invite a friend?
Il y aura beaucoup de monde?	Will there be a lot of people?
Je regrette, mais ce soir, je ne peux pas.	I'm sorry, but tonight I can't.
Je suis très occupé(e) en ce moment.	I'm really busy at the moment.
Demain soir, je serai libre.	I'll be free tomorrow night.

Often, at Higher Level, you are expected to negotiate an arrangement, or to offer alternative suggestions:

Dis, il y a un film super cette semaine. – Ce soir, j'ai quelque chose à faire. Demain, c'est possible?	Look, there's a super film on this week. – I've things to do tonight. How about tomorrow?
Je n'aime vraiment pas les films d'aventures. – Alors, on va voir un film comique? – D'accord.	I really don't like adventure films. – Let's go and see a comedy, then. – OK.
Tu préfères aller au concert ou au théâtre?	Would you prefer to go to the concert or to the theatre?

You will also have to express opinions, and at the highest level to give reasons for or justify your opinions:

Je n'ai pas aimé la pièce. Les acteurs n'étaient pas très bons, et l'histoire n'était pas intéressante.	I didn't like the play. The actors weren't very good, and the plot wasn't interesting.
Ce film était trop long. – Moi, je ne suis pas d'accord. Je l'ai trouvé très émouvant, surtout à la fin.	That film was too long. – I don't agree. I found it very moving, especially at the end.

Rapports personnels, activités sociales et rendez-vous

A Accept or reject the invitations:

1 Tu veux venir au cinéma avec moi? (1)

2 On va au concert ce soir? (1)

3 Tu voudrais venir au café? (1)

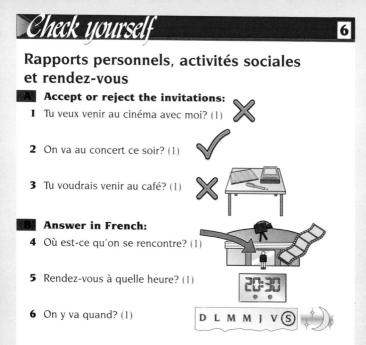

B Answer in French:

4 Où est-ce qu'on se rencontre? (1)

5 Rendez-vous à quelle heure? (1)

6 On y va quand? (1)

C Ask in French:

7 Do you like westerns? (2)

8 Would you like to come to Marie's party? (2)

9 Did you find the film funny? (2)

D Say in French:

10 The film was quite good, but Gérard Depardieu is not my favourite actor. (2)

11 I'd rather stay at home and watch television. (2)

12 I don't much like pop music, and the concert ends too late. (2)

13 I hate violent films. You see too much violence on the TV. (2)

Always accept or refuse politely, never just using *Oui* or *Non*.
1 Je regrette, je ne peux pas. (1)

2 Oui, je veux bien. (1)

3 Non, j'ai des devoirs à faire. (1)

It's more useful to use a full sentence.
4 On se rencontre devant le cinéma. (1)
We tend to say 'outside', but the French use *devant*.
5 Rendez-vous à vingt heures trente. (1) The French use the 24-hour clock much more than the British.
6 On y va samedi soir. (1) There is no need for a word for 'on' here.

Asking questions is a very important skill.
7 Tu aimes/Aimes-tu/Est-ce que tu aimes (1) les westerns? (1)

8 Tu voudrais venir (1) à la boum de Marie? (1)
Remember to use the infinitive for the second of two verbs, and to express the 'apostrophe s' by using *de*.
9 Tu as trouvé (1) le film amusant? (1)
Note how to ask a question in the past. You could also (especially in writing) use *Est-ce que tu as trouvé* or *As-tu trouvé*.

Any error in **either** underlined section means maximum 1 mark.
10 Le film était assez bon, mais Gérard Depardieu n'est pas mon acteur préféré. (2)
Use the imperfect tense for descriptions. Misplacing the negative (*ne ... pas*) with *est* is a very common error.
11 Je préfère rester à la maison regarder la télévision. (2)
Try not to translate your ideas word by word into French, but to use expressions you are familiar with . Note *regarder* – 'and' followed by a verb is often a simple infinitive in French.
12 Je n'aime pas beaucoup la musique pop, et le concert finit trop tard. (2)
13 Je déteste les films violents. On voit trop de violence à la télé. (2) Just because the adjective looks like English, don't forget to make it plural. Don't use *sur* with *télé* – and the French never say *TV*!

La ville et les régions

J'habite une ville	I live in a town
un village	in a village
à la campagne	in the country
à la montagne	in the mountains
au bord de la mer	at the sea-side
dans le nord	in the north
le sud	south
l'est	east
l'ouest	west
le nord-est	north-east
dans le centre	in the centre
de la France	of France
de l'Angleterre	of England
dans le centre-ville	in the town centre
à vingt minutes de	20 minutes from ...
à trente kilomètres de ...	30 kilometres from ...
non loin de ...	not far from ...
Il y a beaucoup	There are a lot
de choses à faire	of things to do
de magasins	of shops
d'habitants	of inhabitants
Il n'y a pas (beaucoup)	There aren't any (many)
de distractions	entertainments
de jeunes	young people
Il y a un complexe sportif.	There is a sports centre.
Il y a deux cinémas.	There are two cinemas.
C'est tranquille	It's quiet
bruyant	noisy
ennuyeux	boring
intéressant	interesting

Le temps

Il pleut.	It's raining.
Il pleut en automne.	It rains in autumn.
Il neige.	It's snowing.
Il neige en hiver.	It snows in winter.
Il gèle.	It's freezing.
Il fait chaud/froid/mauvais.	It's hot/cold/miserable.
Il fait du soleil/du vent.	It's sunny/windy.
Il y a du brouillard/des éclaircies.	It's foggy./There are sunny spells.

GOING FURTHER

In this topic there are many ways of improving your performance from good Foundation to Higher Level.

1 Use adjectives to add more detail:

une ville industrielle	an industrial town
une région touristique	a tourist area

2 Use longer sentences:

J'habite à York, une ville touristique dans le nord de l'Angleterre.	I live in York, a tourist town in the north of England.

3 Introduce a contrast:

La ville est moins paisible, mais il y a plus de distractions qu'à la campagne.	The town is not as peaceful, but there are more entertainments than in the country.

4 Make sure you express plenty of personal opinions:

J'aime habiter à ..., c'est un village pittoresque.	I like living in ..., it's a picturesque village.

5 Don't just answer questions, ask some of your own:

Quel temps fait-il chez toi en été?	What's the weather like where you live in summer?

6 Don't just stick to the present tense; talk about the past and the future too.

J'habite à ... depuis quatre ans.	I've lived in ... for four years.
Mes parents habitaient à Manchester.	My parents used to live in Manchester.
Je voudrais habiter à Londres.	I'd like to live in London.
Il va pleuvoir cet après-midi.	It's going to rain this afternoon.
Elle achètera une maison à la campagne.	She will buy a house in the country.
Il y aura un bal au village ce soir.	There will be a dance in the village tonight.

La ville, les régions, le temps

Say in French:

1 I live in the country. (1)
2 There aren't many shops. (1)
3 York is 40 kilometres from Leeds. (1)

Quel temps fait-il?

1

2

3

(1)   (1)   (1)

Say in French:

7 There is nothing to do in the evening. (2)
8 My sister lives in a quiet village. (2)
9 Southampton is a port in the south of England. (2)

Say in French:

10 I used to live in the mountains, but now I live by the sea. (2)
11 Last week I went to town with my friends, to do some shopping. (2)
12 It's a tourist town, and there will be lots to do in summer. (2)
13 I would prefer to live in Spain, because it's much warmer than in England. (2)

ANSWERS & TUTORIALS

A

1 J'habite à la campagne. (1)
  Je loses its *e* before *h*.
2 Il n'y a pas beaucoup de magasins. (1)
  Note where to put *ne* (*n'* before a vowel).
3 York est à quarante kilomètres de Leeds. (1) Put *à* before the
  distance when saying how far away a place is.

B

4 Il pleut. (1)

5 Il fait du vent. (1)

6 Il y a du brouillard. (1) It's important to remember which of
  the three kinds of expressions (*il fait*, *il y a* or a simple verb)
  to use for each type of weather.

C

7 Il n'y a rien à faire (1) le soir. (1)
  No need for 'in' in French. Note also: *le matin* = in the
  morning; *l'après-midi* = in the afternoon.
8 Ma sœur habite un village (1) tranquille. (1)
  Adjectives usually come after the noun.
9 Southampton est un port (1) dans le sud de l'Angleterre. (1)
  Remember that countries usually have a definite article (*le*,
  la, *l'*, *les*) in French.

D Any error in **either** underlined section means maximum 1 mark.

10 <u>J'habitais</u> à la montagne, mais maintenant <u>j'habite</u> au bord
   de la mer. (2) Use link words (*et*, *mais*, *puis*, *donc*) to create
   longer sentences.
11 La semaine dernière <u>je suis allé(e)</u> en ville avec mes ami(e)s
   <u>pour faire des courses</u>. (2) Adding details such as when or
   with whom you did something adds interest.
12 C'est une ville touristique, et <u>il y aura</u> beaucoup de choses à
   faire <u>en été</u>. (2) You would not use *aller* with the infinitive here.
13 <u>Je préférerais habiter</u> en Espagne, parce qu'il fait <u>plus chaud
   qu'en</u> Angleterre. (2) For giving reasons, *parce que* is a very
   important construction. Notice the *en* before *Angleterre* (than
   in England).

28   **TOTAL**

Il y a une pharmacie près d'ici?	Is there a chemist's near here?
Où se trouve l'hôtel le plus proche?	Where is the nearest hotel?
Où est la gare?	Where is the station?
La boucherie est à cinq minutes.	The butcher's is five minutes away.
La banque est à côté de la librairie.	The bank is next to the bookshop.
Il y a un restaurant au coin, en face de la boulangerie.	There is a restaurant on the corner opposite the baker's.
Le magasin est fermé le lundi.	The shop is closed on Mondays.
Le supermarché est ouvert de neuf heures à dix-neuf heures.	The supermarket is open from 9 a.m. to 7 p.m.
Je cherche un cadeau pour mon frère.	I'm looking for a present for my brother.
Quelle taille?	What size?
Quelle pointure?	What size? (shoes only)
Je peux l'essayer?	Can I try it on?
Vous avez des chemisiers rouges?	Do you have any red blouses?
Il est trop long/court/cher.	It's too long/short/expensive.
Je voudrais une jupe blanche.	I'd like a white skirt.
Elle est trop longue/courte/chère.	It's too long/short/expensive.
Elle ne me va pas.	It doesn't suit me.
Vous l'avez dans d'autres couleurs?	Do you have it in other colours?
Oui, nous l'avons aussi en vert.	Yes, we also have it in green.
Je vous fais un paquet-cadeau?	Shall I gift-wrap it for you?
Les vêtements ne m'intéressent pas.	I'm not interested in clothes.
J'adore la mode.	I love fashion.
Je voudrais un kilo de poires, s'il vous plaît.	I'd like a kilo of pears, please.
Je regrette, nous n'avons pas de petits pois.	I'm sorry, we don't have any peas.
Et avec ça?	Would you like anything else?
C'est tout?	Is that all?
Oui, c'est tout, merci.	Yes, that's all, thank you.
Je voudrais envoyer une carte postale en Angleterre.	I'd like to send a postcard to England.
C'est combien pour envoyer une lettre?	How much is it to send a letter?
Donnez-moi deux timbres à un franc quatre-vingts.	Give me two 1F 80 stamps.

Où est le rayon des vêtements (hommes/femmes/enfants)?

Where is the (men's/women's/children's) clothing department?

L'alimentation est au sous-sol.

The food department is in the basement.

Vous trouverez les fromages là-bas, à côté des surgelés.

You'll find the cheese over there, next to the frozen food.

Ouvert de huit heures à vingt heures, sans interruption.

Open from 8 a.m. to 8 p.m. non-stop.

Le week-end, je vais en ville avec ma mère pour acheter des vêtements.

At the weekend I go into town with my mother to buy clothes.

Avec mon argent de poche, j'achète des CD.

With my pocket money, I buy CDs.

La semaine dernière, j'ai acheté cette montre ici.

I bought this watch here last week.

Elle ne marche pas.

It doesn't work.

Mes parents m'ont donné ce jean comme cadeau d'anniversaire.

My parents bought me these jeans for my birthday.

Il y a un trou.

There's a hole in them.

Il est déchiré.

They're torn.

Ce n'est pas la bonne couleur/taille.

It's not the right colour/size.

Je voudrais envoyer ce colis en Irlande, le plus rapidement possible.

I'd like to send this parcel to Ireland as quickly as possible.

J'ai seulement un billet de cinq cents francs.

I only have a 500 franc note.

J'ai besoin de pièces de un franc.

I need some one franc coins.

Je voudrais changer un chèque de voyages.

I'd like to change a traveller's cheque.

Vous avez une pièce d'identité?

Do you have any identification?

J'ai laissé ma serviette dans le train.

I left my briefcase on the train.

Elle est en cuir marron.

It's made of brown leather.

Dedans, il y avait mes clés, mes lunettes et de l'argent.

Inside, there were my keys, my glasses and some money.

On m'a volé mon portefeuille, il y a dix minutes, dans la rue.

My wallet was stolen ten minutes ago, in the street.

J'ai aussi perdu une bague en or.

I've also lost a gold ring.

Les courses, les services publics

A Find six different items in the word-search:
($\frac{1}{2}$ mark each)

C	V	T	R	S	T	T	O	S
H	L	I	C	L	M	O	S	A
E	O	M	K	G	J	M	U	N
M	S	B	A	N	A	A	P	C
I	C	R	A	V	A	T	E	I
S	A	E	T	E	L	E	P	E
F	R	A	I	S	E	S	N	S
S	T	A	P	T	E	F	L	E
I	E	P	H	E	L	D	V	S

(3)

B Complete each of these sentences with one of the words above:

7 Je voudrais un _____ à un franc quarante. (1)

8 Donnez-moi un kilo de _____ . (1)

9 Avez-vous cette _____ en trente-six? (1)

C Answer in French:

10 Pouvez-vous décrire votre sac à main? (2 détails) (2)

11 Qu'est-ce qu'il y avait dedans? (2 détails) (2)

12 Où et quand l'avez-vous perdu? (2)

D Say in French:

13 that you would like six stamps for England. (2)

14 that the trainers you bought yesterday are too small. (2)

15 that this camera doesn't work and you'd like your money back. (2)

16 that you are not interested in fashion. (2)

A TIMBRE   CARTE   VESTE
FRAISES   TOMATES   CRAVATE (3)

B You often need to use your common sense as well as your knowledge of French.

7 Je voudrais un TIMBRE à un franc quarante. (1)

8 Donnez-moi un kilo de FRAISES/TOMATES. (1)
Either is likely.

9 Avez-vous cette VESTE en trente-six? (1)
Ties don't come in size 12, so it must be a jacket!

C There are often tasks, especially in speaking or writing, where you can choose the details for yourself. In some ways this makes it easier. However, you do have to make sure that the details you give fit the situation, and don't contradict each other – don't arrange to have lunch at six o'clock! Finally, if you are asked to give a certain number of details, make sure you do. Usually, if you are asked for three details about what someone is wearing, you can say three different items of clothing, or two items and a colour, for example *un jean et un T-shirt noir*.

10 Il est en cuir (1) gris (1). It could be in blue plastic, but it does have to be *il* (to go with *sac*).

11 Il y avait cent francs (1) et mon passeport (1) dedans.
Whatever you choose for the contents, make sure it fits with a handbag – not an overcoat, for example.

12 Je l'ai perdu dans le métro (1) ce matin (1).
The answer to 'when?' doesn't have to be a time – *hier* or *ce soir* will often do as well.

D Any error in **either** underlined section means maximum 1 mark.

13 Je voudrais six timbres pour l'Angleterre. (2)
Remember the *l'*.

14 J'ai acheté ces baskets hier. Ils sont trop petits. (2)

15 Cet appareil-photo ne marche pas. Pouvez-vous me rembourser? (2)
Always ask politely, even when you are complaining.

16 Je ne m'intéresse pas à la mode. (2)
Or you could say *La mode ne m'intéresse pas.*

Pardon, monsieur/madame.
Pour aller à la mairie, s'il vous plaît?

Où est la station de métro?
C'est près d'ici?/C'est loin?
Il faut prendre le bus.
C'est la ligne dix.
C'est à dix minutes à pied.
Vous allez tout droit.
Aux feux, vous tournez à droite.
Prenez la deuxième à gauche.
Je me suis égaré(e).
Je cherche le Café des Sports.
On va en ville à pied?

Je voudrais un aller simple pour Dijon.
Un aller-retour pour Dieppe, s'il vous plaît.
Donnez-moi un carnet (de tickets).
A quelle heure arrive/part le car?

Le train pour Lyon part de quel quai?
Je peux réserver une place?
Est-ce qu'il faut changer?
Non, c'est un train direct.
C'est bien le car pour Valence?
Cette place est libre?
Vos billets/passeports, s'il vous plaît.

Le plein de sans-plomb.
Vingt litres de super.
Cinquante francs de gazole.
Vous acceptez les cartes de crédit?
Vous vendez des cartes routières?
Voulez-vous vérifier l'eau/l'huile/la pression des pneus?

Excuse me (to a man/woman)
How do I get to the town hall, please?

Where is the underground station?
Is it near here?/Is it far?
You have to get the bus.
It's a number 10 (bus).
It's ten minutes walk.
You go straight on.
At the traffic lights, you turn right.
Take the second on the left.
I'm lost.
I'm looking for the Café des Sports.
Shall we walk to town?

I'd like a single to Dijon.

A return to Dieppe, please.

Give me a book of (ten) tickets.
What time does the coach arrive/leave?
What platform does the Lyon train leave from?
Can I reserve a seat?
Do I have to change?
No, it's a through train.
Is this the right coach for Valence?
Is this seat free?
Tickets/passports, please.

Fill it up with lead-free.
20 litres of super.
50 francs worth of diesel.
Do you take credit cards?
Do you sell road maps?
Will you check the water/oil/tyre pressure?

Le train numéro mille cent cinquante quatre en provenance de Morlaix entre en gare, quai numéro sept.

Train number 1154 from Morlaix is arriving at platform seven.

Vol AF cent vingt-neuf à destination de Londres. Embarquement immédiat, porte numèro huit.

Flight AF 129 to London. Boarding immediately, gate 8.

Pour aller à la piscine, il y a un bus tous les quarts d'heure.

To go to the swimming baths, there is a bus every quarter of an hour.

Mon moyen de transport préféré c'est l'avion. On arrive tellement plus vite.

My favourite means of transport is flying. You get there so much more quickly.

Moi, je prends plutôt le train. C'est moins rapide, mais plus confortable.

I'd rather go by train. It's not as quick, but it's more comfortable.

J'ai horreur de prendre le bateau, car je souffre du mal de mer.

I dread going by boat, as I get sea-sick.

Partir en voiture, c'est beaucoup plus pratique. On part quand on veut, on s'arrête où on veut.

Going by car is much more convenient. You leave when you like, you stop where you like.

J'ai peur de prendre l'avion, et il y a toujours des retards.

I'm frightened of flying, and there are always delays.

Pour les petits trajets, on devrait aller à pied ou à vélo. C'est moins cher et moins polluant que la voiture.

For small journeys, one should walk or go by bike. It's cheaper and causes less pollution than a car.

Et en plus, on peut éviter les embouteillages.

And what's more, you can avoid traffic jams.

Ma voiture est tombée en panne.

My car has broken down.

Je suis sur la RN seize, entre X et Y.

I'm on the RN16, between X and Y.

C'est une Citroën anglaise. Elle est verte.

It's an English Citroën. It's green.

Le numéro d'immatriculation est L123 SMP.

Its registration number is L123 SMP.

Vous pouvez m'aider?

Can you help me?

Il y a eu un accident.

There has been an accident.

Est-ce qu'il y a des blessés?

Is anyone injured?

La route, les voyages et les transports

A **Match the French with one of the pictures:**

1 Prenez la première à droite. (1)
2 Au rond-point, continuez tout droit. (1)
3 Tournez à gauche après la banque. (1)

A 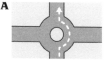 **B**

C  **D**  **E**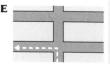

B **Ask in French:**

4 for a single ticket to Marseille. (1)
5 what time the train to Calais leaves. (1)
6 for thirty-five litres of lead-free petrol. (1)

C **Say in French:**

7 I'd like to book three seats on the 2 o'clock coach to Paris. (2)
8 Is there a flight to Manchester tomorrow morning? (2)
9 I'll be arriving at the station at 11.20 on Saturday. (2)

D **Say in French:**

10 To get to town, there is a bus every twenty minutes. (2)
11 I like going by boat. It's not very fast, but it's comfortable. (2)
12 I like going by train, but you often arrive late. (2)
13 I always go by coach. It's much cheaper. (2)

1 C (1)   **2** A (1)   **3** D (1)

4 Je voudrais un aller simple pour Marseille. (1)
You can't leave out the *aller* as you might in English.

5 A quelle heure part le train pour Calais? (1)
Use *pour* (to) before the destination, rather than *à*.

6 Donnez-moi trente-cinq litres de sans-plomb. (1)
You could equally correctly say *Je voudrais* here, but **not**
Avez-vous. (You don't ask a garage if it has any petrol!)

7 Je voudrais réserver trois places (1) dans le car de deux
heures pour Paris (1). Remember this meaning of *places*.
Don't forget the little words *dans* (not *sur*), *de* and *pour*.

8 Il y a un vol pour Manchester (1) demain matin? (1)

9 Je vais arriver à la gare (1) à onze heures vingt samedi. (1)
You could say *J'arriverai*. Remember, no word for 'on' with
days of the week.

Any error in **either** underlined section means maximum 1 mark.

10 <u>Pour aller en ville</u>, il y a un bus <u>toutes les vingt minutes</u>. (2)
Use the infinitive after *pour*. Since *minutes* is feminine, *toutes*
must agree.

11 <u>J'aime prendre le bateau</u>. <u>Ce n'est pas très rapide, mais</u>
c'est confortable. (2) Use the infinitive for the second of a
pair of verbs. When using a negative, it's important to get
the order of words correct.

12 J'aime prendre le train, mais <u>on arrive</u> <u>souvent en retard</u>. (2)
Use *on* when English uses 'you' meaning people in general.
Remember, *souvent* never comes between the subject and the
verb, always after the verb.

13 <u>Je prends toujours</u> le car. C'est <u>beaucoup moins cher</u>. (2)
Like *souvent*, *toujours* comes after the verb. 'Cheaper' in
English is usually *moins cher* in French.

TOTAL

L'ENSEIGNEMENT SUPERIEUR, LA FORMATION ET L'EMPLOI

Je voudrais quitter l'école.	I'd like to leave school.
Je vais retourner au collège.	I'm going to come back to school.
Après le bac, j'espère trouver un emploi.	After the bac ('A' levels) I hope to find a job.
Je vais continuer mes études.	I'm going to continue my education.
Je veux étudier les langues.	I want to study languages.
Je ne veux pas aller en fac(ulté).	I don't want to go to university.
Ma sœur est étudiante à l'université de Toulouse.	My sister is a student at Toulouse University.
J'ai étudié les sciences.	I studied sciences.
Je voudrais devenir ingénieur.	I'd like to be an engineer.
C'est un métier intéressant.	It's an interesting job.
Je ne voudrais pas être vétérinaire.	I wouldn't like to be a vet.
Je n'aime pas les animaux.	I don't like animals.
C'est trop fatigant.	It's too tiring.
Ce n'est pas bien payé.	It's not well paid.
Je ne voudrais pas travailler dans un magasin.	I wouldn't like to work in a shop.
Je voudrais bien travailler avec les enfants.	I'd love to work with children.
Mon frère est au chômage.	My brother is unemployed.
Il cherche un emploi dans un garage.	He's looking for a job in a garage.
Ma mère travaille dans une usine.	My mother works in a factory.
Mes parents sont employés de banque.	My parents work in a bank.
J'ai un petit job le week-end.	I have a little job at the weekend.
Je travaille dans une boutique.	I work in a shop.
Je fais du baby-sitting.	I baby-sit.
Je livre le lait/les journaux.	I deliver milk/newspapers.
J'ai fait un stage dans un bureau.	I did work experience in an office.
Je réponds au téléphone.	I answer the phone.
Je travaille le vendredi soir.	I work on Friday nights.
Je travaille de six heures à dix heures.	I work from six till ten.
Je gagne trente francs de l'heure.	I earn 30 francs an hour.
Je fais des économies.	I put some money away.

Si je réussis à mes examens, je voudrais aller à l'université.

If I succeed in my exams, I'd like to go to university.

Je voudrais apprendre d'autres langues.

I'd like to learn other languages.

Pour devenir médecin, il faut étudier pendant sept ans.

To be a doctor, you have to study for seven years.

J'ai l'intention de travailler dans l'informatique.

I intend to work with computers.

Je voudrais faire une licence de langues, alors je vais faire un stage à l'étranger.

I'd like to do a degree in languages, so I'll have to do work experience abroad.

Mon oncle m'a offert un emploi, donc j'ai décidé de quitter l'école.

My uncle has offered me a job, so I've decided to leave school.

Mon frère est chef de cuisine, mais je ne voudrais pas faire ça – c'est trop fatigant.

My brother is a chef but I wouldn't like to do that – it's too tiring.

Mon ambition, c'est d'ouvrir une boutique de mode.

My ambition is to open a fashion shop.

Je préférerais travailler …
… avec le grand public
… en plein air.
… avec les enfants handicapés.
… avec les autres.
Je n'aimerais pas travailler …
… dans un hôpital
… dans une grande entreprise.

I'd prefer to work …
… with the general public
… in the open air.
… with handicapped children.
… with other people.
I wouldn't like to work …
… in a hospital
… for a large firm.

Qu'est-ce que tu vas faire dans la vie?

What are you going to do for a living?

Je ne sais pas encore – ça dépend de mes résultats.

I don't know yet – it depends on my results.

Je voudrais être informaticien(ne), mais il faut être bon(ne) en maths.

I'd like to work in Information Technology, but you have to be good at maths.

Mon père est au chômage depuis trois ans. Il était ingénieur.

My father has been unemployed for three years. He was an engineer.

Je voudrais être actrice, mais ce n'est pas un emploi très sûr.

I'd like to be an actress, but it's not a very secure job.

L'enseignement supérieur, la formation et l'emploi

A **Answer in French:**

1 Où est-ce que tu travailles? (2)

2 Tu gagnes combien? (2)

3 Tu travailles combien d'heures? (2)

B **Choose a suitable beginning for each sentence:**

4 … parce que c'est bien payé, et on peut aider les malades. (2)

5 … car j'aime rencontrer des gens – et j'adore les maths. (2)

6 … pour voir le monde, car je suis bon(ne) en français. (2)

A Je vais devenir hôtesse de l'air …

B Je voudrais être médecin …

C Je voudrais devenir informaticien …

D Je vais être infirmière …

E J'ai décidé de devenir journaliste …

F Je vais travailler dans une banque …

C **Say in French:**

7 I'd like to be a vet, but you have to be good at sciences. (2)

8 I wouldn't like to work with animals. (2)

9 I've decided to go to university after my exams. (2)

10 I want to be a chef, so I have found a job in a restaurant. (2)

A

1 Je travaille dans (1) un magasin de vêtements (2).
You could use *une boutique* here.

2 Je gagne (1) vingt-cinq francs de l'heure (2).
If you had *par heure*, that's fine.

3 Je travaille de dix-sept heures à vingt et une heures. (2)
It would be OK to use *cinq heures* and *neuf heures*, but the French use the 24-hour clock more often than we do.

B To get these answers right, you need to understand both bits of the answer, as well as the job.

4 B (2) Nurses help the sick, but are not often thought to be well-paid.

5 F (2) Computer operators are good at maths, but meeting people is not usually one of the advantages of the job.

6 E (2) Air hostesses see the world, but they need to be good at foreign languages (not just French).

C Any error in **either** underlined section means maximum 1 mark.

7 <u>Je voudrais être</u> vétérinaire, mais <u>il faut être bon</u> en sciences. (2)

8 <u>Je n'aimerais pas travailler</u> avec <u>les animaux</u>. (2)
You must have *les* in French.

9 <u>J'ai décidé d'aller</u> en faculté <u>après mes examens</u>. (2)

10 <u>J'ai l'intention de devenir</u> chef de cuisine, alors <u>j'ai trouvé</u> un emploi dans un restaurant. (2)
Note: *Je voudrais/j'aimerais/j'ai l'intention de* are more or less interchangeable and, like *j'ai décidé de* and *il faut*, they are followed by the infinitive.

Quel est votre numéro de téléphone?	What is your phone number?
Mon numéro est le deux cent cinquante-sept, zéro huit, quatre-vingt-treize.	My number is two five seven, zero eight, nine three. (257 08 93)
Allô, Mme Lemaître à l'appareil.	Hello, Mrs Lemaître speaking.
Qui est à l'appareil?	Who's speaking?
Je voudrais parler au directeur.	I'd like to speak to the manager.
Ne quittez pas.	Hold the line.
Je vous le/la passe.	I'm putting you through to him/her.
Elle est occupée.	She is busy.
Il n'est pas là en ce moment.	He's not here at the moment
Je peux lui donner un message?	Can I give her/him a message?
Vous pouvez me rappeler?	Can you call me back?
Je rappellerai plus tard.	I'll call back later.
J'ai laissé un message sur le répondeur.	I've left a message on the answering machine.
Elle peut me contacter au ...	She can contact me on ...
Il y a une cabine téléphonique là-bas.	There is a telephone box over there.
Il faut des pièces de un franc.	You need one-franc coins.
Je n'ai pas de monnaie.	I haven't got any change.
J'ai une télécarte /carte de téléphone.	I have a phone card.
Décrochez le combiné et attendez la tonalité.	Pick up the receiver and wait for the dialling tone.
Quel est l'indicatif pour l'Angleterre?	What's the code for England?
Vous composez le zéro zéro quarante-quatre.	You dial 00-44.
Ce soir à vingt et une heures: concours de boules.	Tonight at 9 o'clock: bowls competition.
Inscrivez-vous à la mairie.	Put your name down at the town hall.
Je n'aime pas les publicités pour la nourriture.	I don't like adverts for food.
Les pubs sont très amusantes.	The ads are very funny.
Il y a une annonce dans le journal.	There's an advert in the newspaper.

J'apprends à envoyer des fax.
I'm learning to send faxes.

Vous pouvez me contacter par courrier électronique.
You can contact me by e-mail.

Le matin, j'écoute les messages sur le répondeur.
In the morning, I listen to the messages on the answering machine.

Je fais aussi des photocopies.
I also do photocopying.

Je suis responsable du courrier.
I'm responsible for the mail.

J'ai vu votre annonce dans le journal d'hier.
I saw your advert in yesterday's paper.

Est-ce que vous voulez remplir un formulaire?
Would you like to fill in a form?

Vous pouvez vous présenter pour un entretien, lundi à dix heures?
Can you come for an interview on Monday at 10 o'clock?

Vous avez déjà fait ce genre de travail?
Do you have any experience of this sort of work?

J'ai déjà travaillé dans un restaurant.
I've worked in a restaurant before.

Pourquoi est-ce que vous vous intéressez à ce poste?
Why are you interested in this job?

Quelles sont les horaires?
What are the working hours?

Quel est le salaire?
What are the wages?

Vous pouvez travailler le week-end/le soir?
Can you work at the weekend/in the evening?

Quand est-ce que vous pouvez commencer?
When can you start?

Vous devrez travailler un dimanche sur deux.
You will have to work every other Sunday.

Les publicités pour les voitures encouragent les conducteurs à rouler trop vite.
Car adverts encourage drivers to go too fast.

Je crois qu'on devrait interdire les publicités pour le tabac/l'alcool.
I think adverts for tobacco/alcohol should be banned.

Beaucoup de publicités présentent une image stéréotypée de la femme.
Many adverts show a stereotyped image of women.

Les publicités pour la nourriture me donnent toujours faim.
Food adverts always make me hungry.

La publicité, les communications et les langues au travail

Write out these phone numbers in figures. (If you can, get a friend to read them out in French.)

1 Zéro quatre, quarante-huit, trente-neuf, cinquante, dix-sept. (1)

2 Zéro un, seize, soixante-douze, onze, vingt et un. (1)

3 Zéro cinq, quatre-vingt-quatorze, quinze, zéro deux, treize. (1)

Match the advert with the product.

You should be able to manage this without your dictionary.

4 Vous aurez les dents encore plus blanches. (1)

5 .... lave plus d'assiettes, plus vite et plus brillantes. (1)

6 Pour des cheveux encore plus propres. (1)

   A   **B**   **C**   **D**   **E**

Say in French:

7 I don't want to work in the evening. (2)

8 I can begin on the 3rd of July. (2)

9 I've worked in an office before. (2)

Tell your friend about your new job:

10 You have to answer the phone and open the mail. (2)

11 You work from Monday to Friday, and every other Saturday. (2)

12 The wages are not very good, but the work is interesting. (2)

13 Next week you are going to learn to use e-mail. (2)

A

1 04 48 39 50 17 (1)

2 01 16 72 11 21 (1)

3 05 94 15 02 13 (1)

B

4 B (1) The key word here is *dents* – you can't rely entirely on *blanches* to get the right answer.

5 D (1) You have to understand *assiettes* and *vaisselle* here – *lave* could easily mislead you.

6 A (1) *Shampooing* is probably easy enough, but you also need to understand *cheveux*.

C

7 Je ne veux pas travailler (1) le soir. (1)
Remember the infinitive for the second verb (and in 8). Don't confuse *ce soir* (this evening) with *le soir* (in the evening).

8 Je peux commencer (1) le trois juillet. (1)
You don't need a word for 'on' with dates.

9 J'ai déjà travaillé (1) dans un bureau. (1) Notice that *déjà* (literally 'already') comes before the past participle.

D   Any error in **either** underlined section means maximum 1 mark.

10 <u>Je dois répondre au téléphone</u> et <u>ouvrir</u> le courrier. (2)
Like *répondre*, *ouvrir* goes with *je dois*, and so must be in the infinitive.

11 Je travaille <u>du lundi au vendredi</u>, et <u>un samedi sur deux</u>. (2)
Both the underlined expressions are well worth learning.

12 Le salaire <u>n'est pas très bon</u>, mais <u>le travail est intéressant</u>. (2)
There are all sorts of ways you can say the first half: *Je ne gagne pas beaucoup*, *Ce n'est pas très bien payé*, or *Le salaire n'est pas énorme*. For the second half, you really should use *travail* and not *emploi* or *job*, since the emphasis is on what you actually do.

13 La semaine prochaine <u>je vais apprendre à utiliser</u> le courrier électronique. (2)
You could use *J'apprendrai*, but it's perhaps less usual. Notice that *apprendre* is followed by *à* before the infinitive.

Je vais en Allemagne pendant les grandes vacances.	I'm going to Germany during the summer holidays.
J'ai passé quinze jours à Nice.	I spent a fortnight in Nice.
Nous nous sommes bien amusé(e)s.	We had a good time.
L'hôtel était très confortable.	The hotel was very comfortable.
J'ai visité beaucoup de sites touristiques.	I visited lots of tourist spots.
Les monuments historiques ne m'intéressent pas.	I'm not interested in historic monuments.
Vous avez deux chambres pour ce soir?	Do you have two rooms for tonight?
Je voudrais une chambre ...	I'd like a room ...
... avec douche/salle de bains/WC.	... with shower/bath/toilet.
... pour deux personnes.	... for two people.
... pour une nuit.	... for one night.
C'est cent cinquante francs la chambre.	It's 150 francs for the room.
Le petit déjeuner est servi de sept heures trente à neuf heures.	Breakfast is served from 7.30 to 9.00.
Ça coûte quarante francs par personne.	It costs 40 francs per person.
Il y a une douche et un téléviseur dans chaque chambre.	There's a shower and a television in every bedroom.
Il n'y a pas de couvertures/draps/serviettes.	There are no blankets/sheets/towels.
Il n'y a pas de savon.	There is no soap.
L'ascenseur ne marche pas.	The lift isn't working
Il y a un parking derrière l'hôtel.	There's a car park behind the hotel.
L'auberge de jeunesse est près de la mairie.	The youth hostel is near the town hall.
Je regrette, le camping est complet.	I'm sorry, the campsite is full.
Il est interdit de faire du feu/faire du bruit/faire la lessive.	You must not make fires/make a noise/do your washing.
Il y a un emplacement près des sanitaires/poubelles.	There is a space near the toilet block/dustbins.
On peut louer des sacs de couchage/des vélos.	One can hire sleeping bags/bikes.

GOING FURTHER

En France, on ne prend pas de petit déjeuner à l'anglaise.

In France they don't eat an English-style breakfast.

La spécialité de la région, c'est la tarte au citron.

The speciality of the area is lemon tart.

Une fondue, c'est fait avec du fromage et du vin blanc.

A fondue is made from cheese and white wine.

Je voudrais réserver une chambre pour la semaine du cinq au onze juillet.

I'd like to book a room for the week from the 5th to the 11th of July.

Pourriez-vous m'envoyer des renseignements sur la région et des brochures?

Could you send me some information about the area, and some brochures?

Il y a des dépliants sur les excursions que vous pouvez faire.

There are leaflets about the excursions you can take.

Mon frère vient de faire un safari en Afrique.

My brother has just been on a safari in Africa.

Je préfère passer mes journées à me bronzer sur la plage, et mes nuits en boîte.

I prefer to spend my days getting a tan on the beach, and my nights in a club.

Je suis fanatique de vacances actives.

I'm mad about activity holidays.

L'année dernière, j'ai fait du canoë-kayak sur l'Ardèche.

Last year I went canoeing on the (river) Ardèche.

L'été prochain, je vais faire de l'alpinisme dans les Alpes.

Next summer, I'm going mountain-climbing in the Alps.

Pendant les vacances, ce que j'aime faire, c'est me détendre.

During the holidays, what I like to do is to relax.

Je voudrais une chambre qui ne donne pas sur la rue – il y a du bruit toute la nuit.

I'd like a room which doesn't overlook the street – there's noise all night long.

La chambre est sale, et on n'a pas changé les draps.

The room is dirty, and the sheets haven't been changed.

Il n'y a pas d'eau chaude, et la douche ne fonctionne pas.

There's no hot water, and the shower doesn't work.

La plage est à cent mètres, mais il faut traverser la route nationale.

The beach is 100 yards away, but you have to cross the main road.

La vie à l'étranger, le tourisme, les coutûmes et le logement

A Ask for a room.

1  (1)

2 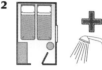 (1)

3  (1)

B Ask in French:

4 ... how much the room is. (1)

5 ... what time dinner is. (1)

6 ... if there is a television in the room. (1)

C Say in French:

7 I want to change my room. It's too noisy. (2)

8 The bed's uncomfortable, and the lavatory doesn't work. (2)

9 My room has not been cleaned. I'd like to see the manager. (2)

D Say in French:

10 What I want to do is to relax by the swimming pool. (2)

11 I hate museums. I think they're boring. (2)

12 I wouldn't like to go on a safari, because I'm afraid of wild animals. (2)

13 I'd love to go water-skiing, but I can't swim. (2)

A You must mention all the details, even if they seem obvious.

1 Je voudrais une chambre pour une personne avec salle de bains. (1)

2 Donnez-moi une chambre pour deux personnes avec douche. (1)

3 Je voudrais une chambre pour une personne pour trois nuits. (1)

B

4 C'est combien, la chambre? (1)
Or you could say *La chambre coûte combien*?

5 Le dîner est à quelle heure? (1)

6 Il y a un téléviseur dans la chambre? (1)
Une télévision would be fine here.

C

7 Je voudrais changer de chambre. (1) Elle est trop bruyante. (1)
Remember to use *elle* (because *chambre* is feminine) and to add the *e* to *bruyante*.

8 Le lit n'est pas confortable, (1) et les WC ne marchent pas. (1)
You can say *inconfortable*, but it isn't always easy to know when you can put *in* in front of an adjective, so unless you actually know the word, it's safer to use *n'est pas*.

9 On n'a pas nettoyé ma chambre. (1) Je voudrais voir le directeur. (1) It is usually easier (and more common) to use *on* in this situation, rather than saying *Ma chambre n'a pas été nettoyée*. Even when complaining, remember to stay polite.

D Any error in **either** underlined section means maximum 1 mark.

10 <u>Ce que je veux faire</u>, c'est <u>me détendre</u> près de la piscine. (2)
Even with the infinitive, you need to use the appropriate reflexive pronoun.

11 Je déteste <u>les musées</u>. <u>Je les trouve</u> ennuyeux. (2) This is easier (and more common) than *Je pense qu'ils sont ennuyeux*.

12 Je <u>n'aimerais pas faire</u> un safari, car <u>j'ai peur des animaux</u> sauvages. (2)
You could say *les animaux sauvages me font peur* instead.

13 Je <u>voudrais bien faire du ski</u> nautique, mais <u>je ne sais pas nager</u>. (2) You need *bien* to give the idea of 'love to'.

TOTAL

Tu es déjà allé(e) aux Etats-Unis?	Have you ever been to the United States?
Je suis allé(e) dans beaucoup de pays européens.	I've been to lots of European countries.
Je ne suis jamais allé(e) en Inde.	I've never been to India.
Je voudrais bien y aller un jour.	I'd love to go there one day.
Quelle est la capitale du Canada?	What is the capital of Canada?
Il y a beaucoup de pays où on parle français.	There are lots of countries where they speak French.
C'est un footballeur français très célèbre.	He's a very famous French footballer.
Elle a gagné une médaille d'argent aux Jeux Olympiques.	She won a silver medal at the Olympic Games.
Il a battu le record de monde.	He broke the world record.
Elle est championne du monde.	She is the world champion.
Il est vedette de cinéma.	He is a film star.
L'Italie a perdu par deux à un.	Italy lost 2-1.
Qui va gagner la Coupe du Monde?	Who's going to win the World Cup?
La pollution, c'est un vrai problème.	Pollution is a real problem.
Il faut protéger l'environnement.	We have to protect the environment.
On doit recycler le verre/le papier.	We ought to recycle glass/paper.
Nous devons conserver l'énergie.	We ought to save energy.
On peut utiliser le vent/le soleil.	We can use the wind/the sun.
On doit éteindre les lumières.	We should turn off lights.
Il faut utiliser moins d'essence.	We have to use less petrol.
Je vais toujours au collège à pied.	I always walk to school.
Les voitures émettent des gaz toxiques.	Cars emit poisonous fumes.
Il faut aussi protéger les animaux sauvages.	We also have to protect wild animals.
Nous devons aussi protéger les forêts.	We have to protect the forests too.

The problems of the environment are very complex, but you should have the vocabulary to say at least something about pollution and conservation, in very simple terms.

On devrait utiliser l'énergie des vagues.	We ought to use wave energy.
L'important, c'est de conserver toutes les ressources naturelles.	The important thing is to conserve all our natural resources.
D'ici trente ans, il n'y aura plus de pétrole.	Thirty years from now, there will be no more oil.
On peut facilement recycler le papier et le verre.	One can easily recycle paper and glass.
Les gaz carboniques émis par les véhicules sont très dangereux.	The carbon gases produced by vehicles are very dangerous.
Les usines aussi produisent beaucoup de gaz toxiques.	Factories also produce many poisonous gases.
C'est très mauvais pour les enfants, surtout les asthmatiques.	It's very bad for children, especially asthmatics.
Aujourd'hui il y a beaucoup plus de maladies respiratoires.	Today there are many more respiratory (breathing) illnesses.
L'air de nos grandes villes est tellement pollué.	The air in our big cities is so polluted.
Il faut interdire aux voitures de circuler en ville.	We must ban cars from driving in towns.
Tout est pollué – l'atmosphère, les océans, les rivières.	Everything is polluted – the atmosphere, the seas, the rivers.
Un autre problème, c'est la pluie acide qui tue les arbes.	Another problem is acid rain, which is killing the trees.
Il y a aussi le réchauffement de la planète – l'effet de serre.	There is also global warming – the greenhouse effect.
Ce qui m'inquiète, c'est le trou dans la couche d'ozone, qui peut causer des cancers.	What worries me is the hole in the ozone layer, which causes cancers.
Nous produisons des tonnes d'ordures, comme les sacs en plastique, et même les déchets nucléaires.	We produce tons of rubbish, such as plastic bags, and even nuclear waste.
On doit penser aux espèces en voie de disparition.	We should think of endangered species.

Check yourself

Le monde

A Find six different countries/languages:

H	A	S	A	R	F	U	E	L	E
P	O	A	N	V	B	I	S	E	A
L	G	L	G	F	E	A	U	S	R
I	T	A	L	I	E	R	I	P	R
P	L	P	E	A	N	G	S	A	L
A	U	R	T	F	N	C	S	G	R
D	S	I	E	I	N	D	E	N	B
C	N	Q	R	K	L	E	A	E	E
B	T	A	R	E	A	R	D	I	S
H	Y	E	E	Q	U	E	C	L	S

(3)

B Say in French:

7 I've never been to Canada. (1)

8 I'd like to go to South Africa one day. (1)

9 They speak French there. (1)

C Correct the errors in these sentences:

10 Les voitures émettent de l'oxygène. (1)

11 Beaucoup d'animaux domestiques sont en voie de disparition. (1)

12 Les sacs en papier sont très dangereux pour les animaux. (1)

13 Un autre problème, c'est le refroidissement de la planète. (1)

14 Au lieu du pétrole, on pourrait utiliser l'énergie de la pluie. (1)

15 Nous devons tous recycler le bois. (1)

These are difficult. Give yourself $\frac{1}{2}$ a mark if you correct the right word(s), even if you don't get it quite right.

D Say in French:

16 We must use less petrol, or there will be no more oil. (2)

17 The greatest danger for the environment is the greenhouse effect. (2)

18 Children have breathing problems because of pollution. (2)

19 Factories emit toxic gases which pollute the atmosphere. (2)

HOLLANDAIS   ANGLETERRE   ESPAGNE
SUISSE   INDE   ITALIE   (3)

7 Je ne suis jamais allé(e) au Canada. (1)
Note that *jamais* comes before the past participle.

8 Je voudrais aller en Afrique du Sud un jour. (1)
With feminine countries, both 'to' and 'in' are *en*.

9 On y parle français. (1) Note that y comes before the verb.

10 Les voitures émettent **des gaz carboniques/toxiques**. (1)
Whatever it is that cars emit, it's not oxygen!

11 Beaucoup d'animaux **sauvages** sont en voie de disparition. (1)
Pets are by definition not endangered species.

12 Les sacs en **plastique** sont très dangereux pour les animaux.
(1) Paper bags are biodegradable (like many scientific words,
it's virtually the same in French: *biodégradable*).

13 Un autre problème, c'est le **réchauffement** de la planète. (1)
Global cooling would be a problem too, but it's not
happening at the moment!

14 Au lieu du pétrole, on pourrait utiliser l'énergie **du
vent/solaire/des vagues**. (1)
Even acid rain isn't an energy source! However, you may
have thought of different examples (*l'hydroélectricité*).

15 Nous devons tous recycler le **verre/papier**. (1)
There are many other things we can recycle, but not wood.

16 Il faut utiliser moins d'essence, (1) ou il n'y aura plus de
pétrole. (1) The phrase *il y a* changes to *il y aura* in the
future (as here) and *il y a eu* in the past.

17 Le plus grand danger pour l'environnement, (1) c'est l'effet
de serre. (1) Remember, *grand* comes before the noun.

18 Les enfants ont des problèmes (maladies) respiratoires (1) à
cause de la pollution. (1) Remember *parce que* has to be
followed by a clause containing a verb.

19 Les usines émettent des gaz toxiques (1) qui polluent
l'atmosphère. (1)

     TOTAL

NOUNS

Masculine or feminine?

There is usually no way to tell, so try to remember nouns together with *un*
or *une*, or *le* or *la*. However, words for male people and animals are normally
masculine (*le taureau* – bull; *un oncle* – uncle), and for female ones normally
feminine (*la vache* – cow; *une tante* – aunt).

Some nouns which refer to people or animals have a different form in the
feminine:

un acteur	*une actrice*	an actress
un directeur	*une directrice*	a manager/headteacher
un serveur	*une serveuse*	a waitress
un vendeur	*une vendeuse*	a shop assistant
un boucher	*une bouchère*	a butcher (also other jobs ending in *-er*: *une boulangère*)
un électricien	*une électricienne*	an electrician (also *informaticienne*, etc)
un chat	*une chatte*	a cat
un chien	*une chienne*	a dog

Plural

Most French nouns make their plural like English ones, by adding *-s*. When
you are listening, this *-s* is always silent, so you need to spot other plural
clues, such as a number (**trois** *cafés*), a possessive (**mes** *frères*) or an article
(**les** *enfants*).
Exceptions:

● Nouns which end in *-s*, *-x* or *-z* don't change in the plural.
● Many nouns which end in *-u* (certainly most of the ones you will meet)
   add *-x* (silent) in the plural. Here are a few examples:

un cadeau	*des cadeaux*	presents
un château	*des châteaux*	castles
un couteau	*des couteaux*	knives
un feu (fire)	*des feux*	traffic lights
un gâteau	*des gâteaux*	cakes
un jeu	*des jeux*	games
un bijou	*des bijoux*	jewels

● Most nouns which end in *-al* make their plural in *-aux*:

un animal	*des animaux*	animals
un cheval	*des chevaux*	horses
un journal	*des journaux*	newspapers

● The plural of *un œil* (an eye) is *des yeux* (eyes).

Articles

These always agree with the noun (masculine/feminine; singular/plural).
un/une (a/an)
These are left out in French when talking about jobs:
Mon frère est chauffeur de camion. – My brother is a lorry driver.
du/de la/de l'/des (some/any)
After a negative, these words become simply *de* (*d'* before a vowel):
Vous avez de la monnaie? – Do you have any change?
Je n'ai pas de monnaie. – I don't have any change.
le/la/l'/les (the)
This is used more often than in English, especially when referring to a
general idea:
Il regarde souvent la télévision. – He often watches television.
Il n'aime pas les haricots verts. – He doesn't like green beans.
à + le/la/l'/les

la boum	Je te vois à la boum.	I'll see you at the party.
le cinéma	On va au cinéma?	Shall we go to the cinema?
l'école	Il est à l'école.	He's at school.
les Pays-Bas	Il habite aux Pays-Bas.	He lives in Holland.

de + le/la/l'/les

le facteur	le camion du facteur	the postman's van
la cuisine	la porte de la cuisine	the kitchen door
l'exercice	la fin de l'exercice	the end of the exercise
les enfants	le ballon des enfants	the children's ball

Adverbs

Just as we can add '-ly' to many English adjectives to form adverbs, we can
do the same by adding *-ment* to the feminine of many French adjectives:
lent → lentement   slow → slowly
However, many common adverbs are not like this:

bien	well		souvent	often
mal	badly		vite	quickly
soudain	suddenly			

Others have slight irregularities:
énorme → énormément   *vrai → vraiment*
évident → évidemment   *récent → récemment*
Unlike in English, adverbs always come after the verb:
Je vais souvent au cinéma. – I often go to the cinema.
However, the adverb often comes before the past participle:
J'ai bien dormi. – I slept well.

Nouns, articles, adverbs

A **Write the French for:**

1 The Italian woman
2 A female chemist
3 The female hairdressers (3)

B **Write in French:**

4 The children
5 (I'd like) some lemonade.
6 (I like) chocolate. (3)

C **Fill in the blanks with** *au/à la/à l'/aux* **or** *du/de la/de l'/des*:

7 J'ai vu le film _____ télé.
8 Voilà la voiture _____ boulangère.
9 On se rencontre _____ café. (3)

D **Complete the unfinished words:**

10 Ma mère est vend_____ dans un magasin de vêtements.
11 J'ai reçu beaucoup de cad_____ pour mon anniversaire.
12 Je n'aime pas les anim_____ . (3)

E **What is missing here?**

13 Je n'ai pas _____ animal.
14 Voilà la fille _____ professeur.
15 Il va _____ école.
16 Ma sœur est _____ secrétaire. (4)

F **Complete the following sentences, using an adverb based on the adjective in brackets:**

e.g. Je l'ai vu _____ . (récent)
Je l'ai vu **récemment**.

17 Elle est partie _____ . (rapide)
18 _____ je l'ai trouvé. (heureux)
19 L'équipe de Marseille a gagné _____ . (facile)
20 Habille-toi _____ , il fait froid. (chaud) (4)

A

1 l'Italienne
2 une pharmacienne
3 les coiffeuses   (3)

Even when you are only writing a few words in French, there is a lot to think about. When using a noun, you always need to ask yourself: 'Is it masculine or feminine, singular or plural, beginning with a vowel?' All these questions need answering before you even consider more complicated things like: 'Does it have a special feminine form?'. One final point; when *italien* is an adjective, or a language, it does not have a capital letter, but when it is a person, it does (as here).
le français – French (the language)
un Français – a Frenchman

B

4 les enfants   5 de la limonade   6 le chocolat   (3)

Remember that the definite article (*le*, etc) is used much more often in French than in English, especially to talk about things in general, as in number 6.

C

7 à la (télé)   8 de la (boulangère)   9 au (café)   (3)

D

10 vend**euse**   11 cad**eaux**   12 anim**aux**   (3)

E

13 Je n'ai pas **d'**animal. Use *d'* after a negative, not *un*.
14 Voilà la fille **du** professeur. Not *de* + *le*.
15 Il va **à l'**école. You need the *l'* in French.
16 Ma sœur est secrétaire. No need for *une* here (with jobs), so there is nothing missing.   (4)

F

17 rapidement The adjective already ends in *-e* so don't add another.
18 heureusement Note feminine of adjectives ending *-eux*.
19 facilement See 17.
20 chaudement   (4)

TOTAL

ADJECTIVES

Position of adjectives

Most adjectives come after the noun:

un métier intéressant – an interesting job

However, there are some exceptions. The following adjectives come before the noun:

beau	beautiful/nice/ handsome/fine	*joli*	pretty
bon	good	*mauvais*	bad
grand	big/tall	*nouveau*	new
gros	fat/big	*petit*	small/little
jeune	young	*vieux*	old

Plural forms

The adjective changes if the noun it describes is plural, usually by adding an *-s*. Here are the exceptions:

● Adjectives which end in *-s* or *-x* do not change in the plural:

les cheveux gris – grey hair   *les vieux livres* – old books

● Adjectives which end in *-u* make their plural in *-x*:

les nouveaux élèves – new pupils

Feminine forms

If the noun is feminine, the adjective changes, usually by adding an *-e*, but again there are some exceptions:

● Adjectives which already end in *-e* do not change in the feminine:

un jeune homme – a young man   *une jeune fille* – a girl

● Adjectives which end in *-if* make their feminine in *-ive*:

sportif → sportive – sporty

● Adjectives which end in *-ien* make their feminine in *-ienne*:

italien → italienne – Italian

● There are some irregular feminine forms:

beau → belle	beautiful (etc)	*gros → grosse*	fat
blanc → blanche	white	*long → longue*	long
bon → bonne	good	*neuf → neuve*	(brand) new
cher → chère	dear	*nouveau → nouvelle*	new
favori → favorite	favourite	*premier → première*	first
gentil → gentille	kind	*vieux → vieille*	old

● Some adjectives do not change in the feminine or the plural:

marron – brown   *les yeux marron* – brown eyes

Possessive adjectives

These come before the noun they describe and, like other adjectives, they change if the noun is feminine or plural:

Masculine	Feminine	Plural	
mon	ma/*mon	mes	my
ton	ta/*ton	tes	your
son	sa/*son	ses	his/her
notre	notre	nos	our
votre	votre	vos	your
leur	leur	leurs	their

*before a vowel

Note that the possessive adjective is masculine or feminine depending on the object involved, not the person:

Jean prend son petit déjeuner. – John is having his breakfast.
Hélène prend son petit déjeuner. – Helen is having her breakfast.

Comparatives

To compare people or objects using adjectives, it is necessary to put *plus*, *aussi* or *moins* in front of the adjective, and *que* after it:

Je suis plus âgé(e) que toi. – I am older than you.
Marie est moins grande que Pierre. – Mary is not as tall as Peter.
Les garçons sont aussi intelligents que les filles. – Boys are as intelligent as girls.

Superlatives

In English, we often make the superlative by adding '-est' to the adjective. In French, it works like the comparative, except that you need to put *le/la/les plus* (or *moins*) in front of the adjective:

Rachid a la plus grande maison. – Rachid has the biggest house.
Le football est le jeu le plus passionnant – Football is the most exciting
du monde. game in the world.

Notice the use of *de* after the superlative:

C'est le garçon le plus intelligent de la classe. – He is the most intelligent boy in the class.

Comparative and superlative of adverbs

This is done just as for adjectives:

Elle parle plus vite que moi. – She speaks more quickly than me.
Les Italiens parlent le plus vite. – The Italians speak fastest.

Adjectives, adverbs

A Complete these sentences, making the adjective agree:

1 J'habite une _____ maison. (grand)
2 Je n'aime pas les chaussettes _____ . (vert)
3 Il a acheté deux _____ CD. (nouveau)
4 Elle va essayer une _____ robe. (beau) (4)

B Add the appropriate possessive adjective (*mon/ton*, etc) in these sentences:

5 Tu veux me prêter _____ stylo?
6 Elle a rencontré _____ amie Claire.
7 Il a perdu _____ clés.
8 Je m'entends bien avec _____ sœur. (4)

C Complete the following French sentences:

9 Marie est _____ _____ _____ Louise.
(Mary is smaller than Louise.)
10 Les garçons sont _____ _____ _____
les filles.
(Boys are not as intelligent as girls.)
11 Je cours _____ _____ _____ toi.
(I run as quickly as you.) (3)

D Complete the following French sentences:

12 C'est la matière _____ _____ _____ .
(It's the most interesting subject.)
13 C'est _____ _____ _____ maison.
(It's the prettiest house.)
14 Hier, c'était le jour _____ _____ _____ .
(Yesterday was the longest day.) (3)

E Say in French:

15 Smith is the fastest player in the world. (2)
16 He is the best looking boy in the class. (2)
17 My sister is older than me. (2)

A

  1 grande
  2 vertes
  3 nouveaux
  4 belle   (4)

If you got any of these wrong, was it because you didn't make the adjective agree, or (3 and 4) because you had forgotten that the adjective was irregular?

B

  5 ton If the subject was *vous*, the possessive would be *votre*.
  6 son Although *amie* is feminine, it begins with a vowel, so not *sa*.
  7 ses Remember, the possessive would be the same if the sentence had begun *Elle a perdu*.
  8 ma   (4)

C

  9 (Marie est) plus petite que (Louise).
 10 (Les garçons sont) moins intelligents que (les filles).
 11 (Je cours) aussi vite que (toi).   (3)

Remember that, while adjectives have to agree, even in the comparative and superlative, adverbs do not.

D

 12 (C'est la matière) la plus intéressante.
 13 (C'est) la plus jolie (maison).
 14 (Hier, c'était le jour) le plus long.   (3)

E

 15 Smith est le joueur **le plus rapide** (1) **du monde**. (1)
     Remember the use of *du/de la*, etc after the superlative.
 16 C'est **le plus beau** garçon (1) **de la classe**. (1)

 17 Ma sœur est **plus âgée** (1) que **moi**. (1)
     Although an adjective ending in *-e* does not change in the feminine, an adjective ending in *-é* does. Note the use of the emphatic pronoun (see PRONOUNS) in comparisons (see also question 11).

TOTAL

PRONOUNS

Subject pronouns

je	I	*nous*	we
tu	you*	*vous*	you
il	he	*ils*	they (masc or mixed)
elle	she	*elles*	they (fem)
on	one (we)		

*to a friend, relative or animal

Object pronouns

me (*m'* before a vowel)	me	*nous*	us
te (*t'* before a vowel)	you	*vous*	you
le (*l'* before a vowel)	him/it	*les*	them (people or things)
la (*l'* before a vowel)	her/it		

Note that all these pronouns come **before** a verb:

Je t'écoute. – I'm listening to you.

lui/leur

These mean 'to him/to her' and 'to them' (though the 'to' is often left out in English):

Je lui ai écrit une lettre. – I wrote him/her a letter.

Nous leur avons parlé. – We spoke to them.

y/en

The pronoun *y* refers to a place:

Tu vas souvent au cinéma? – Do you often go to the cinema?

J'y vais demain. – I'm going (there) tomorrow.

The pronoun *en* refers to a quantity:

Vous avez des frères? – Do you have any brothers?

J'en ai deux. – I have two (of them).

Note that in English, we almost always leave out these words.

Position of pronouns

If you need to use more than one of these pronouns with a verb, there is a fixed order in which they must be used:

1 subject pronoun (There can only be one of these with any verb.)
2 *me te nous vous*
3 *le la l' les*
4 *lui leur*
5 *y*
6 *en*

Maman, où est mon argent de poche? – Mum, where's my pocket money?

Je te l'ai déjà donné. – I've already given it to you.

Emphatic pronouns

moi   *toi*   *lui*   *elle*   *nous*   *vous*   *eux*   *elles*

These are used in a number of ways:

● To emphasise the pronoun:

Je ne sais pas, moi. – I don't know.

● In short phrases where there is no verb:

J'aime bien le cinéma. Et toi? – I love the cinema. How about you?

● After *que*:

Ils sont plus riches que nous. – They are richer than us.

● After prepositions:

après vous – after you   *avant toi* – before you   *avec lui* – with him

de vous – from you   *pour nous* – for you   *sans elles* – without them

● With *c'est*:

C'est moi! – It's me!

● With commands:

Passe-moi le sel, s'il te plaît. – Pass me the salt, please.

● To indicate who something belongs to:

Cette valise est à moi. – This suitcase is mine.

Relative pronouns

● *Qui* is always the subject of the verb which follows it:

Où est la boîte qui contient l'argent? – Where is the box which contains the money?

● *Que* is always the object of the verb which follows it:

Voilà la femme que j'ai vue hier. – There's the woman (whom) I saw yesterday.

● *Ce qui* and *ce que* are used when the pronoun is linked to two different verbs:

Dis-moi ce qui va se passer. – Tell me what is going to happen.

Je ne comprends pas ce que tu as dit. – I don't understand what you said.

● *Lequel/laquelle/lesquels/lesquelles* are used after prepositions. They must agree with the noun to which they refer:

Voici la maison dans laquelle je suis né(e). – Here is the house I was born in.

They combine with à and de as follows:

auquel	*à laquelle*	*auxquels*	*auxquelles*
duquel	*de laquelle*	*desquels*	*desquelles*

● All the above words can refer to people or objects.

Pronouns

A **Complete these sentences:**

1 C'est mon meilleur ami. Je _____ vois tous les jours.
   (He's my best friend. I see him every day.)

2 Où sont les chips? Tu _____ as mangées?
   (Where are the crisps? Have you eaten them?)

3 Pour l'anniversaire de maman, je _____ ai donné des fleurs.
   (For Mum's birthday, I gave her some flowers.)

4 Voici un cadeau. Je _____ ai choisi moi-même.
   (Here is a present. I chose it myself.)

5 Tu aimes le Maroc? – Je ne sais pas, je n'_____ suis jamais allé.
   (Do you like Morocco? – I don't know. I've never been.)

6 Il adore les bonbons. Il _____ a pris six.
   (He loves sweets. He took six.)   (6)

B **Fill in the blanks:**

7 Tu veux venir au cinéma _____ ?
   (Do you want to come to the cinema with me?)

8 Je déteste le football. _____ ?
   (I hate football. How about you?)

9 C'est la cravate de Philippe? – Non, elle est _____ .
   (Is it Philip's tie? – No, it's mine.)

10 Il est nul en sciences, _____ .
   (*He's* useless at science.)   (4)

C **Fill in the blanks with *qui/que/ce qui/ce que*:**

11 Voilà la voiture _____ j'ai vue hier.

12 Montre-moi _____ est dans ta poche.

13 Où est la clé _____ ouvre cette porte?

14 Parle-moi de _____ tu as fait la semaine dernière.   (4)

D **Say in French:**

15 I gave it to you this morning. (2)

16 Describe what you do on Saturdays. (2)

17 Give me your plate. (2)

A

1 le Remember that the same pronoun is used in French to refer to masculine singular **objects**, not just people: *J'adore mon jean vert. Je le porte tous les samedis.*

2 les

3 lui If in English you **could** sensibly put 'to' before 'him' or 'her', in French you **must** use *lui*.

4 l' Before a vowel, both *le* (as here) and *la* become *l'*.

5 y There is no equivalent of *y* in English, so it is very easy to forget to use it. It is used to refer to a place.

6 en Again, no English equivalent. *En* is used to refer to a quantity. (6)

B Note these uses of emphatic pronouns:

7 avec moi After a preposition.

8 Et toi? In a phrase which does not contain a verb.

9 à moi Again after a preposition (*à*), used here in a particular way, to indicate to whom something belongs.

10 lui To stress the person concerned. (4)

C

11 que Because it refers to the object of *j'ai vue*.

12 ce qui The object of *montre* and the subject of *est*.

13 qui The subject of *ouvre*.

14 ce que The object both of *parle* and of *tu as fait*. (4)

D

15 Je te l'ai donné (1) ce matin. (1) Note the order of the pronouns, and their position **before** *ai*.

16 Décris ce que (1) tu fais le samedi. (1) Use *ce que* because 'what' is the object of both *décris* and *fais*. Note that if you were talking to someone you didn't know very well, you would use *vous* – *Décrivez ce que vous faites.*

17 Donne-moi (1) ton assiette. (1) Note the use of the emphatic pronoun *moi* with the imperative. The polite form would be *Donnez-moi votre assiette.*

INDEFINITES

Indefinite adjectives

autre (other):
Tu as un autre stylo? – Do you have another pen?
tout/toute/tous/toutes (all/every):
toutes les quinze minutes – every 15 minutes   *tous les enfants* – all the children
même (same):
Elle aime la même musique. – She likes the same music.
chaque (each):
Répondez à chaque question. – Answer each question.
quelque/quelques (some/a few):
Attendez quelques instants. – Wait a few moments.
plusieurs (several):
J'ai plusieurs photos. – I have several photos.
n'importe quel/quelle (any):
à n'importe quelle heure – at any time

Indefinite adverbs

n'importe comment (no matter how):
Il le fait n'importe comment. – He does it anyhow (ie he takes no care).
n'importe où (anywhere):
Tu peux dormir n'importe où. – You can sleep anywhere.

Indefinite pronouns

n'importe qui (no matter who):
Tu peux parler à n'importe qui. – You can speak to anybody.
quelque chose (something):
Je cherche quelque chose pour ma mère. – I'm looking for something for my mother.
quelqu'un (someone/somebody):
J'ai vu quelqu'un dans le jardin. – I saw someone in the garden.
autre/autres (other):
Va chercher les autres! – Go and get the others!
quelques-uns/quelques-unes (some):
Je n'aime pas les bonbons, mais j'en ai – I don't like sweets, but I ate some.
mangé quelques-uns.
tous/toutes (all):
On y va tous. – Let's all go.
plusieurs (several):
Elle en a plusieurs. – She has several (of them).
chacun/chacune (each):
Je vous donne dix francs chacun. – I'll give you ten francs each.
pas grand-chose (not much):
Il n'y a pas grand-chose à faire. – There isn't much to do.

DEMONSTRATIVES & INTENSIFIERS

Demonstrative adjectives

ce (cet*)/cette/ces (this/that/these/those):
(*before a masculine singular noun beginning with a vowel)
ce journal – this/that newspaper   *cet événement* – this/that event
cette femme – this/that woman   *ces enfants* – these/those children
It is rarely necessary to distinguish between 'this' and 'that' or 'these' and
'those', but if you have to, you can add *-ci* or *-là* to the end of the noun:
ce livre-ci – this book   *ce stylo-là* – that pen
ces robes-là – those dresses   *ces garçons-là* – those boys

Demonstrative pronouns

celui/celle/ceux/celles are used to distinguish between two similar people or
objects:
Je voudrais des cartes postales, – I'd like some postcards,
celles à trois francs.   the ones at three francs.
Tu sais, ce baladeur, celui que j'ai acheté – You know that walkman, the one
la semaine dernière?   I bought last week?
Again, if you really need to make a difference between 'this' and 'that', or
'these' and 'those', you can use *celui-ci* or *celui-là*, etc.
When no noun is specified, use *cela* (often shortened to *ça*) or *ceci*:
Qui a dit ça (cela)? – Who said that?

Intensifiers

The following indicate how much the quality expressed by an adjective or
an adverb is true:
très (very):   *Elle n'est pas très contente.* – She's not very pleased.
trop (too):   *Il court trop vite.* – He runs too quickly.
assez (quite):   *Ma chambre est assez petite.* – My room is quite small.
tellement (so):   *Elle était tellement fâchée.* – She was so angry.
si (so):   *Il est si inquiet.* – He is so worried.
The following indicate how completely the action of a verb is achieved:
tout à fait (completely):
Je n'ai pas tout à fait compris. – I didn't quite understand.
presque (almost/nearly): *J'ai presque fini.* – I've almost finished.
beaucoup (a lot/very much): *Elle travaille beaucoup.* – She works a lot.
These words (as well as *pas beaucoup*, and *pas tout à fait*) can stand alone as
an answer to a question:
Tu as fini? Pas tout à fait. – Have you finished? Not quite.

Demonstratives, indefinites, intensifiers

A **Use one of the following to complete each blank:**

autre   l'autre   les autres   chacun(e)   chaque   même
n'importe comment   n'importe où   n'importe quel(le)   n'importe qui
quelque(s)   quelque chose   quelqu'un   quelques un(e)s
tous   pas grand-chose   plusieurs

1 Répondez à _____ question. (Answer each question.)

2 Je voudrais un _____ café. (I'd like another coffee.)

3 Il porte la _____ veste que moi.
(He's wearing the same jacket as me.)

4 Je peux te rencontrer _____ . (I can meet you anywhere.)

5 Vous avez _____ pour le mal de gorge?
(Do you have something for a sore throat?)

6 Il n'y a _____ à faire. (There isn't much to do.)

7 Patientez _____ instants, s'il vous plaît.
(Hold on a few moments, please.)

8 Voici Pierre et Hélène, mais où sont _____ ?
(There are Pierre and Hélène, but where are the others?)   (8)

B **Complete these French sentences:**

9 Je n'ai pas vu _____ film. (I haven't seen that film.)

10 _____ animaux sont dangereux.
(Those animals are dangerous.)

11 Vraiment, _____ jupe ne me va pas.
(Really, this skirt doesn't suit me.)

12 Qui est _____ enfant? Je ne le connais pas.
(Who is that child? I don't know him.)   (4)

C **Say in French:**

13 I'm not going out this afternoon, I'm too tired. (2)

14 I am so pleased. You are all here. (2)

15 There is someone in that house. (2)

16 There are several children in that family. (2)

A

1 Répondez à **chaque** question. Here 'each' is an adjective describing 'question'; *chacun(e)* is a pronoun, therefore you can't use it here.

2 Je voudrais un **autre** café. You will also hear *Je voudrais encore un café*, but *autre* in this context is becoming more usual.

3 Il porte la **même** veste que moi.

4 Je peux te rencontrer **n'importe où**. It might help to think of these phrases with *n'importe* as meaning 'it doesn't matter where/who/which' etc. You will rarely need to use them, but understanding them could make a difference in reading or listening.

5 Vous avez **quelque chose** pour le mal de gorge? Note that *quelque chose* is two words in French.

6 Il n'y a **pas grand-chose** à faire.

7 Patientez **quelques** instants, s'il vous plaît. This word often has the implication of 'not many' (a few).

8 Voici Pierre et Hélène, mais où sont **les autres**? (8)

B

9 ce

10 ces

11 cette

12 cet Use *cet* before a masculine singular noun beginning with a vowel. (4)

C

13 Je ne sors pas cet après-midi (1), je suis trop fatigué(e). (1) Notice the use of *cet* before a masculine singular noun beginning with a vowel.

14 Je suis tellement content(e). (1) Vous êtes tous là. (1) You could use *si* instead of *tellement*. The French use *là* more often than *ici*, but *ici* would be correct. Remember that in speech, the final *-s* of *tous* would be pronounced.

15 Il y a quelqu'un (1) dans cette maison-là. (1) This is one of those occasions where you might wish to be specific, and to add *-là* to the noun, meaning 'that house over there'.

16 Il y a plusieurs enfants (1) dans cette famille. (1)

NUMBERS

1	*un*	6	*six*	11	*onze*	16	*seize*
2	*deux*	7	*sept*	12	*douze*	17	*dix-sept*
3	*trois*	8	*huit*	13	*treize*	18	*dix-huit*
4	*quatre*	9	*neuf*	14	*quatorze*	19	*dix-neuf*
5	*cinq*	10	*dix*	15	*quinze*	20	*vingt*

21	*vingt et un*	30	*trente*
22	*vingt-deux*	40	*quarante*
23	*vingt-trois*	50	*cinquante*
	etc	60	*soixante*

70	*soixante-dix*	100	*cent*
71	*soixante et onze*	101	*cent-un*
72	*soixante-douze*	200	*deux cents*
73	*soixante-treize*	201	*deux cent un*
	etc	999	*neuf cent quatre-vingt-dix-neuf*
79	*soixante-dix-neuf*	1 000	*mille* (no word for 'a')
80	*quatre-vingts*	2 000	*deux mille*
81	*quatre-vingt-un*	1999	*mille neuf cent quatre-vingt-dix-neuf*
82	*quatre-vingt-deux*		*OR dix-neuf cent quatre-vingt-dix-neuf*
83	*quatre-vingt-trois*		
	etc		
90	*quatre-vingt-onze*	1 000 000	*un million*
91	*quatre-vingt-douze*	1 000 000 000	*un milliard* (a billion)
92	*quatre-vingt-treize*		
	etc		
99	*quatre-vingt-dix-neuf*		

● Remember not to use a comma (1,000, etc) as in French this represents the decimal point:
27.5% in English is 27,5% (*vingt-sept virgule cinq pour cent*) in French.

● 1st *premier (première)* 2nd *deuxième* 3rd *troisième*
  4th *quatrième* 5th *cinquième* 9th *neuvième*

● Telephone numbers are usually paired in French:
03 69 44 83 12 = *zéro trois, soixante-neuf, quarante-quatre, quatre-vingt-trois, douze.*

All French telephone numbers have 10 digits. If you need to say an English phone number which has an odd number of digits, say the first zero separately, and pair the rest:
01592 300158 = *zéro quinze, quatre-vingt-douze, trente, zéro un, cinquante-huit.*

QUANTITIES, DATES, TIME

Quantities

● Whether using metric measures (*un kilo*, *un litre*) or other quantities (*une boîte* [a box/tin], *une bouteille* [a bottle], *un paquet* [a packet], etc), remember to put *de* between the quantity and the item:

Je voudrais un paquet de chips. – I'd like a packet of crisps.

● It is useful to be able to express your own height and weight in metric:

Je mesure un mètre soixante-cinq. – I'm 5 feet 6 (approx).

Je fais cinquante-trois kilos. – I weigh 8 stone (approx).

Dates

● The months do not usually have a capital letter:

| janvier | février | mars | avril | mai | juin | juillet |
| août | septembre | octobre | novembre | décembre |

● For a date, use *le*, followed by a number from 2 to 31, followed by the month. You do not need a word for 'on':

le huit mai – (on) the 8th of May

If it is the first of the month, use *le premier*:

le premier novembre – (on) the 1st of November

● Note the following:

Je vais en ville le samedi. – I go to town on Saturdays.

Je voudrais réserver une chambre du – I'd like to book a room from the
neuf au vingt-trois juillet.   9th to the 23rd of July.

Time

● The easiest way to express the time is by using a number + *heures* + another number to indicate the minutes, if necessary:

Il arrive à onze heures. – He's arriving at 11 o'clock.

Le train part à dix-neuf heures vingt-cinq. – The train leaves at 19.25.

● The 24-hour clock is commonly used in France. However, you may hear the following expressions:

midi – midday

minuit – midnight

onze heures et quart – quarter past eleven

sept heures moins le quart – quarter to seven

neuf heures et demie – half past nine

● Note the present tense of the verb in the following:

J'apprends le français depuis cinq ans. – I've been learning French for five years.

Depuis can also mean 'since':

Je suis là depuis quatre heures. – I've been here since four o'clock.

18

Numbers, quantities, dates, time

A Write out these numbers in words:

1 15
2 48
3 176
4 1994
5 (tél) 03 51 73 11 72
6 (tél) 00 44 114 523789   (6)

You will only need to spell numbers from 1 to 10 – for the rest you can simply write them in figures. However, it is important to know numbers thoroughly, as they are probably the least understood part of the listening test and can lose you significant marks.

B Say in French:

7 half a litre of milk
8 a packet of coffee
9 a bottle of red wine
10 a tin of apricots   (4)

C Complete these French sentences:

11 J'arriverai en France _____ .
    (I'll be arriving in France on the 7th of July.)
12 Je vais en ville _____ .
    (I go to town on Saturdays.)
13 Mon anniversaire, c'est _____ .
    (My birthday is on the first of June.)
14 Je t'attendrai à la gare _____ .   (4)
    (I'll meet you at the station at 8.15 pm.)

D Say in French:

15 I'd like a room from the 30th of August to the 4th of September. (2)
16 I've been studying German for three years. (2)
17 I'll see you at quarter to eleven. (2)

71

A

1 quinze
2 quarante-huit
3 cent soixante-seize There is no word for 'a' or 'one' in front of *cent*.
4 mille neuf cent quatre-vingt-quatorze If it was the year 1994, this could be said *dix-neuf cent quatre-vingt quatorze*.
5 zéro trois, cinquante et un, soixante-treize, onze, soixante-douze French telephone numbers are usually said (and written) in pairs.
6 zéro zéro, quarante-quatre, cent quatorze, cinquante-deux, trente-sept, quatre-vingt-neuf It is best to keep codes (*les indicatifs*) separate from the basic number. (6)

B

7 un demi-litre de lait
8 un paquet de café
9 une bouteille de vin rouge
10 une boîte d'abricots

Remember to use *de* after all expressions of quantity. (4)

C

11 J'arriverai en France **le sept juillet**. No need for a word for 'on'.
12 Je vais en ville **le samedi**. The use of *le* with a day implies 'usually'.
13 Mon anniversaire, c'est **le premier juin**. Dates use a simple number, except for the first of the month.
14 Je t'attendrai à la gare **à vingt heures quinze**. The French often use the 24-hour clock, as here, but you could say *à huit heures et quart*. (4)

D

15 Je voudrais une chambre (1) du trente août au quatre septembre. (1) Note that 'from ... to' is *du ... au* with dates (but *de ... à* with times.)
16 J'étudie l'allemand (1) depuis trois ans. (1) Note the use of the present tense with *depuis*.
17 Rendez-vous à (1) onze heures moins le quart. (1) When you are saying a time, you can always use the 24-hour clock (here, that would be *dix heures quarante-cinq*).

PREPOSITIONS

about   *au sujet de* (on the subject of):
Je veux te parler au sujet des vacances. – I want to talk to you
about the holidays.

vers (approximately):
Il part vers sept heures. – He's leaving about 7 o'clock.

before   *avant:*
Je vais prendre une douche avant le dîner. – I'm going to have a
shower before dinner.

déjà (already):
J'ai déjà vu ce film. – I've seen this film before.

by   *à* (means of transport):
à bicyclette/vélo/moto – by bicycle/bike/motorbike
en (means of transport):
en auto/autobus/avion/bateau/car/ – by car/bus/plane/boat/coach/
train/voiture   train/car
par:
Il a été tué par un camion. – He was killed by a lorry.

for   *pendant* (time during which):
J'ai travaillé pendant deux heures. – I worked for two hours.
pour (time in the future):
J'irai en Italie pour une semaine. – I'll go to Italy for a week.

in   *à* (with names of towns/cities):
à Londres – in London
au (with names of countries which are masculine):
au pays de Galles – in Wales
aux (with names of countries which are plural):
aux Etats-Unis – in the USA
en (with names of most countries):
en France – in France

on   *à:*
à droite/à gauche/à pied – on the right/on the left/on foot
à la télévision/à la radio – on television/on the radio
dans (with means of transport):
J'ai laissé mon sac dans le car. – I left my bag on the coach.
en:
en vacances – on holiday
sur:
sur la table – on the table

73

CONJUNCTIONS & INTERROGATIVES

Conjunctions
These are very useful to create longer, more complex sentences.

alors	so	*car*	for (because)	*donc*	so, therefore
et	and	*mais*	but	*parce que*	because
ou	or	*quand*	when	*si*	if

● *Quand* is often used with a future tense:
Je te téléphonerai quand j'arriverai. – I'll phone you when I arrive.
● *Si* is followed by either the present or the imperfect tense:
Si tu travailles, tu réussiras. – If you work, you will succeed.
Si je partais maintenant, j'arriverais à temps. – If I left now, I would arrive on time.

Interrogatives
There are three ways of asking a question:
● by inversion:
   As-tu cent francs? – Do you have 100 francs?
● by using *est-ce que*:
   Est-ce que tu as cent francs? – Do you have 100 francs?
● by using a rising tone of voice (speech only):
   Tu as cent francs? – Do you have 100 francs?
Many questions are introduced by special words:
Combien (How much/How many):
Combien d'argent gagnes-tu? – How much money do you earn?
Comment (How):
Comment est ton petit ami? – What's your boyfriend like?
Comment t'appelles-tu? – What's your name?
Où (Where):
Où allons-nous? – Where are we going?
Pourquoi (Why):
Pourquoi fais-tu ça? – Why are you doing that?
Quand (When):
Quand allez-vous arriver? – When will you arrive?
Qui (Who):
Qui va m'aider? – Who is going to help me?
Que (What):
Que fais-tu? – What are you doing?
Qu'est-ce que (What):
Qu'est-ce qu'on fait maintenant? – What shall we do now?
Quel:
Quel âge as-tu? – How old are you?   *Quelle est la date?* – What's the date?
Qu'est-ce qui (What):
Qu'est-ce qui se passe? – What's happening?

Prepositions, conjunctions, interrogatives

A Choose suitable conjunctions to link these parts of sentences:

1 Ma voiture est en panne, _____ je suis venu en train.
2 Je dois partir, _____ le bateau part bientôt.
3 Il déteste le français, _____ il n'aime pas les maths non plus.
4 Je lui ai dit bonjour _____ il est entré.
5 Je voudrais venir en France, _____ je n'ai pas assez d'argent.
6 Tu prends une glace _____ une crème caramel?   (6)

B Here are the answers. What were the questions?

7 Je m'appelle Luc.
8 Je gagne quarante francs de l'heure.
9 Il veut travailler en France pour améliorer son français.
10 Nous avons passé les grandes vacances à Toulouse.
11 J'arriverai chez vous lundi matin.
12 J'aime les films d'épouvante.   (6)

C Choose an appropriate preposition to complete each of these sentences:

13 Je veux te parler _____ tes examens.
(I want to talk to you **about** your exams.)
14 Je vais partir en Italie _____ quelques jours.
(I'm going to go to Italy **for** a few days.)
15 J'ai vu le match _____ la télévision.
(I saw the match **on** television.)
16 Mes parents ont une petite maison _____ pays de Galles.
(My parents have a little house **in** Wales.)   (4)

D Say in French:

17 What are you going to do this weekend? (2)
18 I don't like sports because they're boring. (2)

SCORE

A

1 **alors** You could use *donc* here, though it's a bit stronger ('therefore' rather than 'so').

2 **parce que** You could also use *car* here.

3 **et** *Mais* would also fit. 'He hates French **but** he doesn't like maths either.'

4 **quand**

5 **mais**

6 **ou** (6)

B

7 **Comment t'appelles-tu?** OR **Tu t'appelles comment?**

8 **Tu gagnes combien?** OR **Combien est-ce que tu gagnes?** Inversion (*Combien gagnes-tu?*) would be correct, but not very usual.

9 **Pourquoi veut-il travailler en France?** You could say *Pourquoi est-ce qu'il veut ....* An alternative (though less likely) question might be: *Qu'est-ce qu'il va faire pour améliorer son français?*

10 **Où avez-vous passé les grandes vacances?** You have to use *vous* here, because it clearly refers to more than one person (*nous*).

11 **Quand est-ce que tu arriveras?** The question *A quelle heure arriveras-tu* would lead to a more definite time than *lundi matin* (on Monday morning).

12 **Qu'est-ce que tu aimes comme films?** You might equally say *Quel genre de film aimes-tu?* (6)

Note that in numbers 7, 8, 11 and 12, *vous* would work as well as *tu*.

C

13 **Je veux te parler au sujet de tes examens.** *Vers* means 'approximately', so would be wrong here.

14 **Je vais partir en Italie pour quelques jours.**

15 **J'ai vu le match à la télévision.** *Sur* = on top of.

16 **Mes parents ont une petite maison au pays de Galles.** (4)

D

17 **Qu'est-ce que tu vas faire** (1) **ce week-end?** (1) You could say *Que vas-tu ....*

18 **Je n'aime pas les sports** (1) **parce qu'ils sont ennuyeux.** (1) You could use *car* instead of *parce que*.

TOTAL

VERBS – PRESENT TENSE

The French present tense is the equivalent of the English 'I speak', 'I am speaking' and 'I do speak'. It works through a system of endings. There are three main types of French verb:

	er	**ir**	**re**
	parl(er) (to speak)	fin(ir) (to finish)	vend(re) (to sell)
je	parle	finis	vends
tu	parles	finis	vends
il/elle/on	parle*	finit*	vend _*
nous	parlons	finissons	vendons
vous	parlez	finissez	vendez
ils/elles	parlent**	finissent**	vendent**

*Use these endings if the subject is a person's name, or any other singular noun.

**Use these endings if the subject is any plural noun.

A few notes on pronunciation:
- The final consonant is not pronounced.
- For each of these verbs, all the singular forms have the same sound.
- For er verbs, the endings -e, -es and -ent are silent.

Spelling notes:
- Verbs ending -yer replace the y with i except before -ons and -ez.
- Verbs ending -ler/-ter often have a double consonant except before -ons and -ez.
- Verbs ending -cer have ç in front of -ons.
- Verbs ending -ger add e in front of -ons.

Reflexive verbs
These are er verbs, with an extra pronoun:
SE COUCHER – to go to bed

je me couche	nous nous couchons
tu te couches	vous vous couchez
il/elle se couche	ils/elles se couchent

Remember that je, te, me, se all lose their e before a vowel or h.

Impersonal verbs
These are only used in the 3rd person singular:

Il gèle. – It's freezing.   Il neige. – It's snowing.   Il pleut. – It's raining.

Il faut – ... must:

Il faut partir. – I/You/We (etc, depending on the context) must leave.

Il y a – There is/There are:

Il y a trois cinémas en ville. – There are three cinemas in town.

Irregular verbs

There are more than 40 irregular verbs you might meet in your GCSE exam. The following are the ones you absolutely must know:

ALLER – to go
je vais
tu vas
il/elle/on va
nous allons
vous allez
ils/elles vont

AVOIR – to have
j'ai
tu as
il/elle/on a
nous avons
vous avez
ils/elles ont
(needed for making the perfect tense)

ETRE – to be
je suis
tu es
il/elle/on est
nous sommes
vous êtes
ils/elles sont

FAIRE – to make/do
je fais
tu fais
il/elle/on fait
nous faisons
vous faites
ils/elles font

PRENDRE – to take
je prends
tu prends
il/elle/on prend
nous prenons
vous prenez
ils/elles prennent
Used with means of transport (to catch), food & drink (to have).
Same as *apprendre* (to learn) and *comprendre* (to understand)

VENIR – to come
je viens
tu viens
il/elle/on vient
nous venons
vous venez
ils/elles viennent

DEVOIR – to have to/must
je dois
tu dois
il/elle/on doit
nous devons
vous devez
ils/elles doivent

POUVOIR – to be able/can
je peux
tu peux
il/elle/on peut
nous pouvons
vous pouvez
ils/elles peuvent

VOIR – to see
je vois
tu vois
il/elle/on voit
nous voyons
vous voyez
ils/elles voient

VOULOIR – to want (to)
je veux
tu veux
il/elle/on veut
nous voulons
vous voulez
ils/elles veulent

SAVOIR – to know (a fact)
je sais
tu sais
il/elle/on sait
nous savons
vous savez
ils/elles savent

Verbs – present tense

Complete the following, using the correct form of these verbs:

quitter – to leave   *remplir* – to fill   *appeler* – to call
commencer – to begin   *attendre* – to wait   *essayer* – to try on

1 Je quitt_____
2 Tu rempl_____
3 Elle appel_____
4 Nous commen_____
5 Vous attend_____
6 Louise et Marie essa_____   (6)

Fill in the blanks with the appropriate verb:

7 Nous _____ trop de chocolat.
(We eat too much chocolate.)

8 Il _____ à sept heures.
(He gets up at 7 o'clock.)

9 Nous _____ de bonne heure.
(We're leaving early.)

10 Ils _____ l'espagnol au collège.
(They learn English at school.)

11 Tu _____ bien avec ta sœur?
(Do you get on well with your sister?)

12 Il est tard. Tu _____ partir.
(It's late. You must go.)   (6)

Say in French:

13 We get washed in the bathroom. (dans la salle de bains)
14 I am going to town on Saturday. (en ville samedi)
15 They want to go to the cinema. (aller au cinéma)
16 We have breakfast in the kitchen. (le petit déjeuner dans
la cuisine)   (4)

Say in French:

17 My friends see their father at the weekend. (2)
18 Can you come and see me tomorrow? (2)

A

1 Je quitt**e**.
2 Tu rempl**is**.
3 Elle appell**e**. Note the double *l*.
4 Nous commen**çons**. Note the cedilla (ç) before *-ons*.
5 Vous attend**ez**.
6 Louise et Marie essa**ient**. Note that the *y* usually
   becomes *i*.   (6)

B

7 Nous **mangeons** trop de chocolat. Don't forget to put in the
   e before *-ons* with verbs ending in *-ger*.
8 Il **se lève** à sept heures. Remember the reflexive pronoun –
   the verb is *se lever* – to get up. Note too the accent on the *e*.
9 Nous **partons** de bonne heure.
10 Ils **apprennent** l'espagnol au collège. Note that *apprendre*
   behaves just like *prendre*.
11 Tu **t'entends** bien avec ta soeur? Another reflexive verb
   (*s'entendre [bien] avec* – to get on [well] with).
12 Il est tard. Tu **dois** partir.   (6)

C

13 Nous nous lavons (dans la salle de bains). Always remember
   the extra pronoun with reflexive verbs (*se laver* – to get
   washed).
14 Je vais (en ville samedi). Remember that in French the simple
   present tense is used for both 'I go' and 'I am going'.
15 Ils veulent (aller au cinéma).
16 Nous prenons (le petit déjeuner dans la cuisine). Don't forget
   that *prendre* has many meanings in addition to 'to take'. In
   particular it is used with food and drink to mean 'to have'.(4)

D

17 Mes copains voient (1) leur père le week-end. (1) Remember
   to use the *-ent* ending after any plural subject, not just *ils*
   and *elles*.
18 Pouvez-vous venir (1) me voir demain? (1) You could equally
   begin *peux-tu*. Note the use of *venir me voir* to mean 'come
   and see me'.

Perfect tense

This is used to refer to events in the past. It is made up of two parts:

● **present tense of *avoir***   OR   **present tense of *être***

j'ai	*nous avons*	*je suis*	*nous sommes*
tu as	*vous avez*	*tu es*	*vous êtes*
il/elle/on a	*ils/elles ont*	*il/elle/on est*	*ils/elles sont*

● PLUS the past participle:

-é (for er verbs)   *-i* (for ir verbs)   *-u* (for re verbs)

Use *avoir* with the majority of verbs, and *être* with the following verbs only:

aller	to go	*partir*	to leave
arriver	to arrive	*rentrer*	to return
descendre	to go down	*rester*	to stay
devenir	to become	*retourner*	to return
entrer	to go in	*revenir*	to come back
monter	to go up	*sortir*	to go out
mourir	to die	*tomber*	to fall
naître	to be born	*venir*	to come

and all reflexive verbs

When using *être* the past participle agrees with the subject – see examples * below.

Some common verbs have irregular past participles:

s'asseoir → assis – sat	*lire → lu* – read	
apprendre → appris – learned	*mettre → mis* – put	
avoir → eu – had	*mourir → mort* – died	
boire → bu – drank	*naître → né* – born	
comprendre → compris – understood	*offrir → offert* – offered	
conduire → conduit – drove	*ouvrir → ouvert* – opened	
connaître → connu – knew	*plaire → plu* – pleased	
croire → cru – thought	*prendre → pris* – took	
courir → couru – ran	*recevoir → reçu* – received	
couvrir → couvert – covered	*rire → ri* – laughed	
devenir → devenu – became	*savoir → su* – knew	
devoir → dû – had to	*tenir → tenu* – held	
dire → dit – said	*venir → venu* – came	
écrire → écrit – wrote	*voir → vu* – saw	
être → été – was	*vouloir → voulu* – wanted	
faire → fait – did		

Examples:

j'ai mangé – I ate	*nous avons bu* – we drank
tu as choisi – you chose	*vous êtes arrivé(e)(s)* – you arrived
il a vendu – he sold	*elles se sont habillées* – they got dressed

VERBS – PAST TENSES

Imperfect tense

This is used to give descriptions in the past. It works through a system of endings:

je	-ais	nous	-ions
tu	-ais	vous	-iez
il/elle/on	-ait	ils/elles	-aient

These endings are added to the *nous* form of the verb without the *ons*:

je mangeais   *tu vendais*   *elle finissait*

The only exception is *être*, which adds the endings on to *ét-*:

j'étais	nous étions
tu étais	vous étiez
il/elle/on était	ils/elles étaient

Pluperfect tense

This is one step further into the past than the perfect tense. It is the equivalent of 'I had ... ' in English. It is formed by using the imperfect of *avoir* or *être* with the past participle:

j'avais mangé – I had eaten   *nous avions bu* – we had drunk
tu avais choisi – you had chosen   *vous étiez arrivé(e)(s)* – you had arrived
il avait vendu – he had sold   *elles s'étaient habillées* – they had got dressed

The use of the past tenses

● To talk about something which has already happened, for example a holiday, most of the verbs you use will be in the perfect tense:

Nous sommes parti(e)s à sept heures du matin. – We left at 7 am.
Nous avons joué sur la plage, et nous sommes – We played on the beach, and
allé(e)s au cinéma. went to the cinema.
J'ai appris à faire la planche à voile. – I learned to windsurf.

● However descriptions, for example of the hotel, need the imperfect:

L'hôtel était très agréable, et les repas – The hotel was very good, and the meals
étaient super. were super.
Le voyage était trop long. – The journey was too long.

● You also use the imperfect for things which happened regularly.

Tous les jours, après le petit déjeuner, nous – Every day, after breakfast, we used
allions à la plage. to go to the beach.

● You may need a pluperfect, to explain what had happened:

Nous nous sommes levé(e)s tard, car nous – We got up late as we had had too
avions trop bu. much to drink.

Verbs – past tenses

A Complete these French verbs in the perfect tense:

1 Je _____ . (arriver)

2 Elle _____ . (réussir)

3 Vous _____ . (entendre)

4 Jeannette _____ . (partir)

5 Nous _____ . (recevoir)

6 Ils _____ . (se coucher) (6)

B Fill in the blanks in the following French sentences with the appropriate verb:

7 Jihane _____ avec sa mère.
(Jihane was talking to her mother.)

8 Nous _____ le film.
(We had seen the film.)

9 Elle _____ avec ses copines.
(She has gone out with her friends.)

10 Nous _____ au cinéma tous les vendredis.
(We used to go to the cinema every Friday.)

11 Ma mère _____ très contente.
(My mother was very pleased.)

12 Il _____ sa chemise jaune.
(He put on his yellow shirt.) (6)

C Say in French:

13 When we returned home, it was raining. (2)

14 They closed the windows and went out. (2)

15 He finished his dinner, which was very good. (2)

16 Everyone was dancing and singing. (2)

A

1 Je suis arrivé(e). If you are female, don't forget to make the past participle agree if the verb uses *être* in the perfect tense.
2 Elle a réussi. However, if the verb uses *avoir* the past participle does not agree.
3 Vous avez entendu.
4 Jeannette est partie. Past participle agrees, because *partir* uses *être*.
5 Nous avons reçu.
6 Ils se sont couchés. Past participle agrees, because reflexive verbs use *être*. (6)

B

7 Jihane **parlait** avec sa mère. 'Was ... ing' in English is always the imperfect in French.
8 Nous **avions vu** le film. Remember that 'had ... ' requires the pluperfect (imperfect of *avoir* or *être* with past participle).
9 Elle **est sortie** avec ses copines. If the verb uses *être* in the perfect, the past participle has to agree.
10 Nous **allions** au cinéma tous les vendredis. The imperfect is used to express the English idea of 'used to ... '.
11 Ma mère **était** très contente. Descriptions in the past need the imperfect.
12 Il **a mis** sa chemise jaune. Many of the most common verbs (like *mettre*) have irregular past participles. (6)

C

13 Quand nous sommes rentré(e)s (1) (à la maison) il pleuvait. (1) The verb *rentrer* is often used on its own (without *à la maison* to mean 'to return home'. The weather in the past will very often be in the imperfect.
14 Ils ont fermé les fenêtres (1), et ils sont sortis. (1) Because one of the verbs uses *avoir* and the other *être*, you have to put both verbs in full. If both used *avoir* (or *être*) you would not need to repeat it: *Il a ouvert la fenêtre et fermé la porte*.
15 Il a fini son dîner (1), qui était très bon. (1) The first verb is what happened (perfect), the second description (imperfect).
16 Tout le monde dansait (1) et chantait. (1) Note that *tout le monde* is singular.

VERBS – FUTURE TENSES

The future

This is used to talk about what will happen. It works through a system of endings. These endings are the same for all verbs, and are added on to the infinitive (for *re* verbs after first removing the final *e*):

je	-ai	*nous*	-ons
tu	-as	*vous*	-ez
il/elle/on	-a	*ils/elles*	-ont

Examples:

je parlerai – I will speak
tu finiras – you will finish
elle vendra – she will sell

nous partirons – we will leave
vous arriverez – you will arrive
ils attendront – they will wait

Although the endings are always the same, some verbs are irregular:

aller → *j'irai* – I will go
avoir → *j'aurai* – I will have
devenir → *je deviendrai* – I will become
devoir → *je devrai* – I will have to
être → *je serai* – I will be
faire → *je ferai* – I will do
pouvoir → *je pourrai* – I will be able
recevoir → *je recevrai* – I will receive
venir → *je viendrai* – I will come
voir → *je verrai* – I will see
vouloir → *je voudrai* – I will want

Notes:

● The future is often used after *quand*:
Je serai là quand tu arriveras. – I will be there when you arrive.

● Just as in English, it is also possible to refer to future events by using the verb 'to go', followed by the infinitive:
Je vais voir mes grands-parents. – I'm going to see my grandparents.
Elle va prendre une tasse de thé. – She's going to have a cup of tea.
Nous allons regarder le match à la télé. – We're going to watch the match on TV.

● Again, as in English, the French quite often use a simple present tense to refer to a future event, if there is a clear indication that it is in the future – such as the use of words like *demain* (tomorrow), *ce soir* (tonight), *la semaine prochaine* (next week), etc:
Ce soir, je vais au cinéma. – Tonight, I'm going to the cinema.
Elle part en vacances la semaine prochaine. – She's going on holiday next week.

The conditional

This is used to talk about what would happen (if something else happened). It often comes in a sentence containing *si* (if). It is formed just like the future, using the following endings:

je	-ais	*nous*	-ions
tu	-ais	*vous*	-iez
il/elle/on	-ait	*ils/elles*	-aient

There are no exceptions.

The most common example of a conditional is *je voudrais* followed by an infinitive:

Je voudrais continuer mes études. – I would like to continue my education.

Other examples:

Si je gagnais à la loterie, j'achèterais – If I won the lottery, I would buy
une belle voiture. a nice car.

Si j'avais 18 ans, je quitterais la maison. – If I was 18, I would leave home.

The future perfect

This is not a very common tense, but you may need to recognise it. It is formed by using the future of *avoir* or *être* with the past participle and is most commonly used after *quand* (when) or *dès que* (as soon as):

Dès que j'aurai fini mes examens, – As soon as I have finished my exams,
je partirai en vacances. I shall go on holiday.

The conditional perfect

Like the future perfect, you will not need to use this, but you may need to recognise it. It is formed by using the conditional of *avoir* or *être* with the past participle.

It is usually used with a *si* clause in which the verb is in the pluperfect, and is the equivalent of '(If something had happened) I would have ... ':

Si je t'avais vu, je t'aurais dit "bonjour". – If I had seen you, I would have said "hello".

S'il avait su qu tu étais en ville, il serait – If he'd known you were in town, he
venu te voir. would have come to see you.

Check yourself

Verbs – future tenses

A Complete these verbs in the future tense:

1 Je _____ (choisir)
2 Tu _____ (aller)
3 Pierre _____ (acheter)
4 Nous _____ (attendre)
5 Vous _____ (pouvoir)
6 Ils _____ (venir)   (6)

B Fill in the blanks with the appropriate verb:

7 Je _____ à la maison à huit heures.
   (I will be at home at 8 o'clock.)
8 Que _____-tu, si tu gagnais à la loterie?
   (What would you do if you won the lottery?)
9 Les enfants _____ au football.
   (The children are going to play football.)
10 _____-vous m'aider, s'il vous plaît?
   (Could you help me, please?)
11 Après l'université, elle _____ vétérinaire.
   (After university, she will be a vet.)
12 Il mangera quand il _____ .
   (He will eat when he arrives.)   (6)

C Say what these sentences mean in English:

13 Quand j'aurai fini mon repas, je sortirai.
14 Si j'étais venu(e), je t'aurais vu.   (2)

D Say in French:

15 They'd prefer to go to the swimming pool tonight. (2)
16 I will wait for you outside the cinema at seven o'clock. (2)
17 When are you going to write to your aunt? (2)

ANSWERS & TUTORIALS

SCORE

A

1. Je choisirai.
2. Tu iras.
3. Pierre achètera. Don't forget to add the accent (è) in the future.
4. Nous attendrons. Remember, with *er* verbs you must drop the *e* from the infinitive before adding the endings.
5. Vous pourrez.
6. Ils viendront. (6)

B

7. Je **serai** à la maison à huit heures.
8. Que **ferais** -tu, si tu gagnais à la loterie? The conditional is often used in a sentence containing a *si* clause.
9. Les enfants **vont jouer** au football. You could say *Les enfants joueront ...* , but this is more natural.
10. **Pourriez** -vous m'aider, s'il vous plaît? The conditional of *pouvoir* is often used as a very polite formula – 'Could you ... ' or 'Would you mind ... '.
11. Après l'université, elle **deviendra** vétérinaire. The verb *devenir* behaves just like *venir*.
12. Il mangera quand il **arrivera**. Unlike in English, the French use the future after *quand* in this sort of sentence. (6)

C

13. When I have finished my meal, I will go out. Literally 'When I **will have** finished my meal ... '.
14. If I had come, I would have seen you. (2)

D

15. Ils préféreraient aller (1) à la piscine ce soir. (1) Notice the accents on the verb. In English, we would often say 'They would rather ... ' for *Ils préféreraient*.
16. Je te verrai (1) devant le cinéma à sept heures. (1) As with the present tense, object pronouns come before the verb in the future.
17. Quand est-ce que tu vas écrire (1) à ta tante? (1) As in 9, this is more natural than *Quand écriras-tu*.

88

TOTAL

The negative

The negative consists of two words (though the *ne* is often left out in speech) which go round the verb:

ne ... pas – not

ne ... jamais – never/not ever

ne ... rien – nothing/not anything

ne ... personne – no-one/not anyone

ne ... plus – no more/no longer

ne ... que – only

ne ... guère – hardly/scarcely

ne ... ni ... ni – neither ... nor

ne ... aucun(e) – not any

ne ... nulle part – nowhere

In the present tense, *ne* goes before the verb, and the other part of the negative after it:

Je n'aime pas le football. – I don't like football.

In the perfect tense, the negative words go round the part of *avoir* or *être*:

Tu n'as jamais vu ce film? – Have you never seen this film?

BUT *Elle n'a vu personne.* – She didn't see anyone.

If there is an object or reflexive pronoun, *ne* goes before it:

Ils ne se lèvent pas de bonne heure. – They don't get up early.

The passive

Elle a été piquée par une guêpe. – She has been stung by a wasp.

This can be tricky, and in any case the French often prefer to use:

Une guêpe l'a piquée. – A wasp stung her.

On lui a volé sa montre. – His watch has been stolen.

Les télécartes se vendent ici. – Phone cards are sold here.

The present participle

This is formed by adding *-ant* to the *nous* form of the present tense without the *ons*. It is used (usually with *en*), to indicate one action taking place at the same time as another:

Elle est tombée en faisant du ski. – She fell while ski-ing.

The subjunctive and past historic

In your exam, you will only meet these in the reading test. The past historic is only ever used in written form and has the same meaning as the perfect tense. The subjunctive is used after expressions like:

il faut que – (one) must

avant que – before

bien que/quoique – although

jusqu'à ce que – until

It is usually clear what the verb is, though there are a few irregular subjunctives:

aller → j'aille

avoir → j'aie/il ait

être → je sois

faire → je fasse

The infinitive

This is the form of the verb usually found in dictionaries, and always ends in *-er*, *-ir* or *-re*. It has four main uses:

1 If there are two verbs together, the second will be in the infinitive:

● These verbs are followed immediately by the infinitive:

adorer – love	*devoir* – have to	*préférer* – prefer
aimer – like	*espérer* – hope	*savoir* – know how to/can
désirer – want to	*il faut* – must	*vouloir* – want to
détester – hate	*pouvoir* – can	

J'espère aller à l'université. – I hope to go to university.

● After the following verbs, the infinitive has *à* in front of it:

aider – help (someone to do something)	*se décider* – make up mind
apprendre – learn	*hésiter* – hesitate
commencer – begin	*inviter* – invite
continuer – continue	*réussir* – succeed

Elle commence à parler. – She is beginning to speak.

● After the following, the infinitive has *de* in front of it:

avoir besoin – need to	*essayer* – try to
avoir peur – be afraid of/to	*finir* – finish
avoir le temps – have time to	*oublier* – forget
cesser – stop	*promettre* – promise
décider – decide	*regretter* – be sorry to
empêcher – prevent from	

Il a décidé de devenir prof. – He has decided to be a teacher.

2 The infinitive is used after *aller* to refer to a future event (see VERBS – FUTURE TENSES).

3 The infinitive is used after *venir de* to express the idea of 'just':
Present: *Elle vient d'arriver.* – She has just arrived.
Imperfect: *Il venait de partir.* – He had just left.

4 The infinitive is used after prepositions:

à	quelque chose à manger – something to eat
après	Après avoir mangé, il est parti. – When he had eaten, he left.
avant de	Mange avant de partir. – Eat before you go.
pour	Je suis là pour voir le film. – I'm here to see the film.
sans	Il est parti sans me dire au revoir. – He left without saying goodbye.

Remember, if there is a pronoun with the infinitive, the pronoun comes first:
Je viendrai te voir demain. – I'll come and see you tomorrow.

Verbs – general

A Use a negative to change the meaning of these sentences:

1 Marie likes strawberries. – Marie aime les fraises.
  Marie doesn't like strawberries. – _____

2 She said hello to me. – Elle m'a dit bonjour.
  She didn't say anything to me. – _____

3 I have a lot of money. – J'ai beaucoup d'argent.
  I have no more money. – _____

4 I saw someone. – J'ai vu quelqu'un.
  I didn't see anybody. – _____

5 We go to bed late. – Nous nous couchons tard.
  We don't go to bed late. – _____

6 I have 100 francs. – J'ai cent francs.
  I only have 100 francs. – _____   (6)

B Fill in the blanks with *à* or *de* if necessary, and the appropriate infinitive.

7 Il apprend _____ . (to drive.)

8 J'ai oublié _____ la porte. (to close)

9 J'espère _____ à l'université. (to go)

10 Pouvez-vous m'aider _____ les lits? (to make)

11 Elle a décidé _____ en Suisse. (to work)

12 Il ne faut pas _____ en retard. (to arrive)   (6)

C Say what these sentences mean in English:

13 Je ne l'aime pas, bien qu'il soit généreux.

14 Il prit le train pour aller à Paris.   (2)

D Say in French:

15 I do my homework while watching television. (2)

16 He had just started when I arrived. (2)

17 We didn't eat anything before we left. (2)

A

1. Marie n'aime pas les fraises.
2. Elle ne m'a rien dit.
3. Je n'ai plus d'argent.
4. Je n'ai vu personne.
5. Nous ne nous couchons pas tard.
6. Je n'ai que cent francs. (6)

As well as knowing the meaning of the different negatives, it is important to put them in the right place.

B

7. Il apprend **à conduire**.
8. J'ai oublié **de fermer** la porte.
9. J'espère **aller** à l'université.
10. Pouvez-vous m'aider **à faire** les lits?
11. Elle a décidé **de travailler** en Suisse. But remember that *se décider* (to make one's mind up to ...) is followed by *à* plus the infinitive.
12. Il ne faut pas **arriver** en retard. The impersonal verb *il faut* can be used for any person – 'I must', 'she must', 'they must', etc. (6)

C

13. I don't like him, although he is generous. The subjunctive of *être* is *soit*.
14. He caught the train to go to Paris. The past historic has the same meaning as the perfect tense. *Il prit* is from the verb *prendre*. (2)

D

15. Je fais mes devoirs (1) en regardant la télévision. (1) Use *en* with the present participle for an action which happens simultaneously with the main verb.
16. Il venait de commencer (1) quand je suis arrivé(e). (1) Use *venir de* in the imperfect to mean 'had just'. In the present it would mean 'have/has just'.
17. Nous n'avons rien mangé (1) avant de partir. (1) Note the position of the negative with a verb in the perfect. Don't try to use *avant que* here – it is never used when both verbs have the same subject.

TOTAL

- Listening is more difficult to practise than reading, partly because you need the right equipment, but mainly because it is hard to find the right sort of things to listen to. Tuning in to French radio might seem like a good idea, but it can be very hard. Why not try the radio or TV broadcasts aimed at 14-16 year-old students of French, or the tape/CD from a course-book or the *Study & Revision Guide*? If it's a bit too easy, that's fine – it will give you practice and confidence. Take every chance you can to listen to people speaking French. Listening really is a case of practice makes ... perhaps not perfect, but certainly much better! Once you have found some listening material, you should practise really listening to it, training yourself to listen for specific information that you know is there.

- Make sure you get your teacher to tell you exactly what sort of questions to expect in the exam. You may not be able to use a dictionary (again, check with your teacher what the rules are for the exam you are doing), so you need to be familiar with the settings and instructions you will need to understand.

- Make sure you answer questions in the right language – look at the instructions and the examples.

Using the dictionary

- Before the test starts:
  - check any instructions you don't understand;
  - check words in the longer phrase or sentence multiple-choice questions;
  - if there is time, check vocabulary for the visuals (though these tend to be the easier items where you should probably know all the vocabulary) so that you can listen for the key-words. Remember that you will only have five minutes, so only check words you really don't know.
  - During the test, jot down words you hear which you don't know – the spelling may not be spot on, but should be close enough.

- After the test:
  - check the words you have jotted down;
  - check any other words you didn't understand on the question paper. Don't rely on the dictionary – learn as much vocabulary as you can.

Some particular problems

Numbers: Even very good candidates can have problems because:
- The numbers you learned as isolated words often do not have the same sound when they are with other words. For example, *trois* sounds very different from *treize*, but *trois amis* can sound quite like *treize amis*. Practise listening to numbers followed by nouns.
- The numbers from 70 to 99 are more complex in French; it is easy to hear *quatre-vingt-dix-huit* and understand 88. Again, the best solution is practice.

The alphabet: Spelling out a name or a place is a very common element of the Listening Test. Most of the names of the letters are very similar to English, but there are some differences:
- The letter **i** is pronounced 'ee' while the letter **e** is pronounced 'euh' (as in *deux*).
- The letter **g** is pronounced '*jé*' while the letter **j** is pronounced 'jee' (both with a soft 'j' sound as in *je*).
- It can be hard to distinguish between **b** (bé) and **p** (pé); **d** (dé) and **t** (té); **m** (emm) and **n** (enn).
- **H** (ash) and **y** (ee-grek) sound quite different from their English equivalents.

Consonants: These are often harder to distinguish than vowels:
- **b/p** *bain* can sound like *pain*;
- **m/n** *mettre* can sound like *naître*;
- **d/t** *dent* can sound like *tend*;
- **f/v** *faire* can sound like *vers*.

Negatives: These are very easy to miss (especially when the speaker is speaking fairly quickly) but they are vital to accurate understanding.
- *Je ne veux pas sortir* is clearly negative when you see it written down, but in normal speech it becomes much closer to *J'veux pas sortir*.

Memory: This can be important in listening.
- In a long conversation, try to keep track of who is speaking.
- Don't be afraid of jotting down a few notes as you listen – but don't let this stop you concentrating on listening.

Useful strategies

- Make sure you take advantage of the pause between items to read the next question.

- If you are asked what time two people will meet, then you are only listening for a time – but be careful, in more difficult questions you may hear more than one time suggested, only one of which is agreed.

- If you are asked where and when they will meet, then you need to put two pieces of information together – and again, if it is a Higher Level question, one of the places or times may be rejected during the conversation.

- If the question asks for an attitude and/or a reason, make sure that you listen out for the speakers saying how they feel. However, although a simple *elle aime* or *il déteste* might be enough in your answer, the French you hear is not likely to contain such phrases. You must be prepared to hear more complex expressions such as *ne peut pas supporter* ('can't bear').

- If the question consists of a number of French phrases, from which you have to choose the most appropriate, try to decide before you hear the French what sort of attitudes the list of phrases represents. That way, you have an idea of the attitudes you are likely to hear.

- If there is an example, make sure you look at it. It will tell you how long your answer should be (a single word, a phrase or a sentence), and whether it is likely to be a verb, a noun or an adjective.

- The questions will almost always be printed in the same order that you will hear the information, especially if there are sub-questions – (a), (b) or (i), (ii), etc. The only exception to this may be when you are asked one general question about the gist of what you have heard (often in the questions in English), when you may need to listen right to the end before you make up your mind.

- Remember that, although the questions in English may look easier, they may be used to test the most complicated sorts of understanding – attitudes, opinions or deductions – working out from a number of (possibly contradictory) statements what the balance of an opinion is.

Higher Level skills

- Understanding French spoken at normal speed. This will include speakers who use colloquial expressions, interrupt each other, or leave sentences unfinished.

- Understanding longer utterances, or conversations between two or more people. Indeed, one quite common type of question is to identify who said what, and this inevitably means three or four different speakers. It may help to jot down a few notes, but don't forget to **listen**. Often, the French you need to understand in these longer utterances is no harder than at lower levels, but the extra skill is in pinpointing the right bit of information.

- Picking out the main points or key ideas. This is often a question of listening to someone giving a number of different examples (*Les billets coûtent au moins cinquante francs, et puis je devrais manger au restaurant, et après, c'est trop tard pour prendre le dernier car, alors il faudrait prendre un taxi*) and working out what point the speaker is making (that it would cost too much).

- Understanding the gist of what is said. In this sort of question, you may well get no credit for picking out all the specific examples. In the utterance outlined above, if the question asked 'How does Jean feel about going to the concert?' the answer 'He can't afford it' or 'He thinks it would cost too much' is a better answer than 'The tickets cost 50 francs, and he'd have to eat at a restaurant and go home by taxi'.

- Answering questions using French you have not heard on the cassette. Again, if the above example had a question in French (*Quelle est l'attitude de Jean?*), you would have to answer something like *C'est trop cher* – though the word *cher* is not on the cassette.

- Understanding vocabulary which is not in the Minimum Core Vocabulary list. Each examining group publishes a list, but this only applies to vocabulary which is tested at Foundation Level. You must expect at Higher to be able to understand more than this. One of the skills of understanding a foreign language is to be able to deduce (guess sensibly) the meaning of an unknown word, using the context to help you.

Listening 1–4

Try to work with a friend, taking turns to read the French out loud.

Pick out the detail from these sentences:

1 J'ai un frère et deux sœurs.	COMBIEN?
2 Si on se rencontre devant le cinéma.	OU?
3 Rendez-vous à la gare à huit heures vingt-cinq.	QUAND?
4 J'ai passé une semaine à Paris avec mes parents.	AVEC QUI? (4)

Complete the grid with the appropriate weather.

Aujourd'hui, vendredi, il fera un temps splendide partout en Bretagne, avec quelques averses seulement sur la côte cet après-midi. Le week-end, par contre, le ciel sera couvert, et le matin il fera plutôt frais. Mais dimanche, à partir de midi, on reverra le soleil.

	Matin	Après-midi
Vendredi		
Samedi	froid	
Dimanche		soleil

soleil   froid   nuages
averses en montagne
averses au bord de la mer
pluie le matin   éclaircies (4)

Indicate for which speaker each phrase is true according to the dialogue. If no information is given, write ? .

– Qu'est-ce que tu vas faire l'année prochaine, Paul?

– Oh, je ne sais pas encore. Si je réussis au bac, je vais étudier des langues à l'université. Sinon, je trouverai un emploi. Et toi, Christian?

– Je vais travailler dans le magasin de mon père. C'est assez intéressant. Mais d'abord, je vais passer quelques semaines au bord de la mer – en Italie, je crois, avant de commencer le travail.

A Il veut travailler à l'étranger.   B Il voudrait continuer ses études.
C Il va partir en vacances.   D Il espère avoir de bons résultats. (4)

How did they feel about their work experience, and why?

A – J'ai choisi de faire mon stage dans un complexe sportif, car je suis assez sportive, mais en fait je n'ai rien fait sauf servir au café. N'importe qui aurait pu le faire – et c'était vraiment ennuyeux!

B – J'ai trouvé mon stage à la dernière minute – dans une banque! Je croyais que j'allais vraiment m'ennuyer, mais au contraire. J'ai appris des tas de choses sur les ordinateurs, et j'ai parlé aux clients. (8)

A In these questions, all you have to do is identify the correct information.

1 1 frère/2 sœurs You need to give both bits of information to gain the mark.

2 devant le cinéma

3 8h 25 The place is given, too, but you only need the time.

4 (avec) parents
(4)

B In this question, you have to match what you hear with the different expressions in the question:

	Matin	Après-midi
Vendredi	**soleil**	**averses au bord de la mer**
Samedi	froid	**nuages**
Dimanche	**froid**	soleil

(4)

temps splendide = soleil   averses sur la côte = averses au bord de la mer
ciel couvert = nuages   plutôt frais = froid (approximately)

C

A ? Although Christian mentions Italy, it's for a holiday, not to work.

B Paul He would clearly like to go to university – if he passes his exams.

C Christian Spending a few weeks by the sea implies a holiday.

D Paul
(4)

D

A Disappointed/upset/displeased (1) You have to deduce this from all the other things she says – it is never explicitly stated.
Wanted to do something connected with sport/to take advantage of being sporty. (1)
Had to work in café. (1)
Found work boring. (1) These three details are clearly expressed, but you have to see that they are reasons for her disappointment.
B Pleased/happy/satisfied/enjoyed it. (1) Again, not explicitly stated.
Wasn't bored/was afraid he would be bored. (1)
Learned about computers. (1)
Dealt with/spoke to customers. (1) Again, you need to work out that these are the reasons he enjoyed the work.
(8)

Role-plays

- Foundation/Higher: You will have visual and/or verbal prompts for each task. Use your dictionary during preparation time to make sure that you have the necessary vocabulary. It might be worth trying to predict the unprepared task – for which you will not have a specific prompt – but make sure that at that point in the test you listen carefully to the teacher.
- Higher: These are harder to prepare, because they usually contain a problem to solve and so they can develop in different ways. The important thing is to read the scene-setting, make sure you understand the situation, and prepare some vocabulary which will be useful. However, a lot depends on reacting appropriately to the teacher. (**NB** The MEG Higher role-play can be prepared in more detail, as it requires you to narrate a series of events in the past.)

Presentation (MEG, NEAB only)

- Choose a topic which:
  - you can do without relying too much on your notes;
  - interests you.

  Make sure that the topic will give you scope for referring to past, present and future events and for expressing personal opinions, and that it will allow you to use a variety of language.
- When you are preparing the presentation, practise timing it (1 minute for MEG, 1½ minutes for NEAB followed by a discussion with the teacher). Make sure that your first sentence says what you are going to talk about: *Je vais parler de ma famille.*
- There is no need to learn your presentation off by heart. Obviously, the first stage will be writing a script, which you will then practise to get the timing and delivery right. However, if you go on from there to trying to deliver it without the script, it will be better than something that you have learnt parrot fashion.
- Have some visual support – photos, etc. They will make it more natural, and will remind you of what to say next.
- Don't try to rush it. Make your delivery as smooth as possible, but don't go any faster than you are comfortable with.

General conversation

● Your teacher will ask questions to get you to refer to past, present and future, but it's up to you to make sure that you do. It isn't enough for the teacher to ask: *Qu'est-ce que tu as fait le week-end dernier?* and for you to reply: *Une promenade à la campagne*. It has to be you who refers to the past, which means using a verb: *J'ai fait une promenade à la campagne*. Listen for questions containing *tu as ...?* or *tu es ...?* with a past participle, and make sure you answer *j'ai ...* or *je suis ...* with the past participle. The same applies to the future. If you hear *tu vas ...* with an infinitive, that's your cue for the future, so answer *je vais ...* with the infinitive.

● Your teacher will also ask questions intended to get you to produce personal opinions. Try to make at least some of your answers a little more complex than *j'aime ...* or *je n'aime pas ...* Use expressions like *je crois que ...* ('I think that ...') or *à mon avis ...* ('in my opinion').

If you don't refer to past, present and future, and express personal opinions, you won't get a Grade C.

To go further, you need to:

● use longer sentences, perhaps linked with *mais*, *alors*, *donc*, *après*;
● use *qui* and *que*;
● use adjectives and adverbs;
● volunteer extra details, without waiting for the teacher to prompt them. For example, if the teacher asks: *Quelle est ta matière préférée?*, don't just reply *J'aime bien les maths*, but go on to say *parce que je trouve ça très intéressant, et le prof, qui s'appelle M. Brown, est sympa*.

You should try **not** to:

● reply very briefly. If a question asks for the answer *Oui* or *Non*, make sure you go on to expand on this. If you are asked: *Tu aimes le sport?*, reply: *Oui, parce que je suis assez bon, et c'est important pour la santé* or *Non, je trouve ça ennuyeux*.

● pause for too long before you answer. A moment to consider your answer is natural, but if you are really having problems, try to produce a short answer, or even *Je ne sais pas* which will encourage your teacher to move on to a different question.

SPEAKING GUIDANCE 3

Pronunciation and intonation

Good pronunciation is something you should have acquired over the years you have been learning French, and not something to swot up in the few days before the test. However, there are things you can do to avoid some of the most common errors.

- Try to get hold of a recording of the French alphabet. It will provide good models for many of the French sounds.
- If you pronounce consonants as you would in English, you won't go far wrong at this level, but there are a few problems:
1 **G** has two sounds: hard, like in 'gun', before *a*, *o* or *u*, or soft, like in the French word *je*, before *e* or *i*.
2 **H** is silent, and words like *le*, *la* and *je* drop their final vowel before it.
3 **Q** (always followed by *u*) makes a sound like *k*.
4 **R** needs a little care. Imitation is the only way of producing it, but it is more prominent than the same letter in English, which is often scarcely pronounced at all.
5 **W** is always pronounced like the letter *v*, except in a few words which have been taken in from other languages, like *western* and *water*.
6 **Y** is always pronounced like the letter *i* – and never like in 'young'.
- Vowels are almost all quite different in sound from their English equivalents. Ask your teacher to go over with you the following words, and use them as a model for your pronunciation:

  a   as in *ma*   **e**   as in *de*   **é**   as in *clé*
  è/ê as in *mère*   **i**   as in *si*   **o**   as in *kilo*
  u   as in *tu*

- Different combinations of letters also affect the sound. Use the following words as models:

  ai – *maison*   **au** – *au*   **eu** – *heure*   **oi** – *soir*
  ou – *sous*   **ui** – *huit*   **an/en** – *dans/dent* **ei** – *reine*
  ain – *bain*   **on** – *ton*   **un** – *brun*   **oin** – *coin*
  in/im – *instant/impact* (but if the consonant is doubled, the sound becomes much more like the English):
  imm/inn – *immédiat/innocent*

SPEAKING GUIDANCE 4

Some common errors in pronunciation

- If the last letter of a word is a consonant, it is usually silent. In this sentence, the silent letters are in brackets:
  Vou(s) voule(z) un gran(d) li(t)?
- Be particularly careful with verbs: with *er* verbs, the forms *(je/il/elle) parle, (tu) parles,* and *(ils/elles) parlent* all sound the same.
- If a word ending in a consonant comes before a word beginning with a vowel, then the final consonant is usually pronounced:
  Il(s) regardent la télé BUT *Ils arrivent demain.*
- The final *r* of a word is often pronounced: *soir; pour.*

Keeping the conversation moving

- If you don't understand the teacher's question, your conversation will seem very hesitant, and even worse, you may answer the wrong question. Make sure you know thoroughly the question words, which give you an instant clue as to what you are being asked:
  Où? – Where? – often confused with:
  Qui? – Who? (also *Avec qui?* – With whom?)
  Quand? – When? – a little less precise than:
  A quelle heure? – At what time?
  Combien? – How much/many?
  Comment? – How?
  Est-ce que ...? This introduces a question which can be answered 'Yes' or 'No' – but which, of course, you should expand on.
  Pourquoi? – Why? You would normally answer this with *parce que.*
- If your teacher wants to encourage you to give an opinion, he or she might ask: *Qu'est-ce que tu penses de ...?* (What do you think of ...?)
- If your teacher wants a full answer, containing plenty of detail and description, he or she might say: *Parle-moi de ...* (Talk to me about ...), or *Fais-moi une description de ....* (Give me a description of ...).
- If you really don't know what to say, encourage your teacher to move on by saying: *Je ne sais pas* or *Je ne comprends pas.* Remember, the more you control the conversation, and the more you say, the less likely this problem is to occur – but don't try to take over and produce a monologue, or your teacher will have to interrupt!

Speaking 1–4
Role-plays

A You go into a lost property office, as you have lost your suitcase. You will have to:
- greet the employee and say why you are there.
- describe the case. (2 details)
- answer a question.
- say when you lost the case
- say what was in the case. (2 details)

1 Saluez l'employé(e) et dites pourquoi vous êtes venu(e).
2 Décrivez votre valise. (2 détails)
3 Répondez à la question: Où avez-vous perdu votre valise?
4 Dites quand vous avez perdu la valise.
5 Dites ce qu'il y avait dans la valise. (2 détails)   (5)

B You have had an accident and go to the hospital.
- Symptômes. (2 détails)
- Accident.
- Où et quand.

Respond to the teacher's questions:
6 Qu'est-ce qu'il y a?
7 Qu'est-ce qui est arrivé?
8 Ça s'est passé où et quand?
9 Je peux contacter quelqu'un? Qui?
10 Quel est le numéro de téléphone?   (5)

C The notes below give an outline of a day during a holiday by the sea. (2 marks each)

11 SE LAVER	A quelle heure?	Petit déjeuner
12 LA PLAGE	Quel temps?	Activités
13 DEJEUNER	Où?	Qu'est-ce qu'on a mangé?
14 APRES-MIDI-EXCURSION	Où?	Avec qui?
15 LE SOIR	Qu'est-ce qu'on a fait? (2 details)	(10)

SCORE

A You could leave out the parts in brackets, as they would probably be in the question.

1 Bonjour, monsieur/madame. J'ai perdu ma valise. You needn't complicate this by trying to say: 'I'm here because ...'.

2 Elle est petite et verte. Remember the agreements – they do make a difference when you say them aloud.

3 (Je l'ai perdue) dans le métro.

4 (Je l'ai perdue) ce matin.

5 (Dans la valise il y avait) des pulls et un jean. This is a minimum for two details. It might be better to add, for example, some adjectives. (5)

B (For brackets, see explanation in **A** above.)

6 J'ai mal au bras et au cou. This is a minimum for two details.

7 Je suis tombé(e) en faisant du vélo. At this level you probably ought to give more detail than just *Je suis tombé*.

8 (Ça s'est passé) au camping ce matin.

9 Oui, vous pouvez téléphoner à ma mère. It is probably better not to repeat *contacter* from the question if you can avoid it.

10 (Son numéro de téléphone est le) cent quatorze, deux cent cinquante-sept, trente-neuf, soixante-trois. (5)

C The following suggestions give you an idea of how much you should say. One mark for each phrase with a different verb, to a maximum of two per item.

11 Nous nous sommes levés à sept heures et demie, et nous avons pris le petit déjeuner au restaurant. (2) You could say what you ate, too.

12 Puis nous sommes allés à la plage, car il faisait chaud. Moi, j'ai nagé et joué au volley. (2) Change from *nous* to *je* adds variety.

13 A midi, nous avons mangé nos sandwichs au bord de la mer. (2) It's OK to be fairly brief here, as long as you expand elsewhere.

14 Après le déjeuner, nous sommes allés au parc d'attractions avec des copains. C'était formidable! (2)

15 Après le dîner, je suis allée en boîte avec Céline, et nous avons dansé. Nous sommes rentrés à l'hôtel très tard, vers deux heures du matin. (2)

TOTAL

Speaking 1–4

General conversation

Answer fairly briefly:

1 A quelle heure commencent les cours dans ce collège?
2 Quels sont tes passe-temps préférés?
3 Qu'est-ce que tu aimes manger au petit déjeuner?
4 Tu as combien de frères et sœurs?
5 Où es-tu allé(e) le week-end dernier? (5)

Answer in a sentence, using a verb:

6 Qu'est-ce que tu as fait hier pour aider à la maison?
7 Que fais-tu d'habitude pendant les vacances de Noël?
8 Qu'est-ce qu'il y a d'intéressant à faire dans ta région?
9 Où est-ce que tu vas aller avec tes copains le week-end prochain?
10 Fais-moi la description de ta chambre. (5)

Answer at length, using at least two verbs, and adding an extra detail to each sentence or phrase.

11 Parle-moi un peu de ta ville/ton village. (2)
12 Fais-moi une description de ton/ta meilleur(e) ami(e). (2)
13 Quel pays est-ce que tu voudrais visiter? Pourquoi? (2)
14 Qu'est-ce que tu vas faire au mois de septembre? (2)
15 Parle-moi un peu des problèmes de la pollution. (2)

A Even here, you could easily add a further detail.

1 A neuf heures moins le quart. *Chaque cours dure une heure.*
2 Le football et la télévision. *J'adore les feuilletons à la télé.*
3 Du pain grillé et des céréales. *Quelquefois je prends un œuf.*
4 Deux frères et une sœur. *Ils sont tous plus âgés que moi.*
5 Au cinéma. *J'ai vu un film d'aventures.* (5)

B To go further, you could always add an opinion.

6 J'ai passé l'aspirateur. *Je déteste faire le ménage.*
7 Je vais voir mes grands-parents. *Je m'entends bien avec eux.*
8 A York, on peut aller dans les musées. *Moi, je trouve ça passionnant.*
9 Je vais voir un match de football samedi. *Arsenal, c'est mon équipe préférée.*
10 Elle est petite et bleue. *Je voudrais une chambre plus grande.* (5)

C One mark for each phrase containing a different verb, up to a maximum of two per item.

11 Mon village se trouve dans le nord de l'Angleterre. Il est assez petit, mais il y a deux ou trois magasins. (2) Remember to use pronouns (*il/elle*) to avoid repetition, and use link words (like *mais*) to create longer sentences.
12 Ma meilleure amie s'appelle Claire. Elle a les yeux bleus et les cheveux blonds. Elle est très sympa. (2) If you said *elle est grande et sympa*, you've only used one verb.
13 Je voudrais aller aux Etats-Unis, car il y a beaucoup de choses à voir, et on y parle anglais. (2) Giving reasons is one of the Higher Level skills.
14 Si tout va bien aux examens, j'espère continuer mes études au lycée. Je voudrais étudier les sciences. (2) Using a clause with *si* is also a Higher Level skill. This would also count as one of your references to the future.
15 Les gaz toxiques émis par les voitures sont très mauvais pour la santé, et le trou dans la couche d'ozone est aussi dangereux. (2) This is a hard topic. Make sure you have the vocabulary to say at least a couple of sentences about it. It's not always easy to get a past reference in this topic. Try something like: *Ma petite sœur est asthmatique. Elle était malade l'hiver dernier à cause de la pollution atmosphérique.*

Using the dictionary

Make sure you can find your way round your own dictionary easily, and that you understand its key abbreviations:

adj. – adjective   sing. – singular   masc. – masculine
adv. – adverb   pl. – plural   fem. – feminine
n. – noun

These are some of the more common ones, but check your own dictionary – it will contain a list of abbreviations used.

1 Look up, and write down the meanings of, the following words (even if you know some of them – this is just a practice):
   a *soucoupe*   **b** *potable*   **c** *composter*   **d** *meuble*   **e** *réveil*

The answers are below. Those words were quite quick to check, because your dictionary probably gives only one meaning for each.

2 Now do the same for the underlined words:
   a *Elle s'est assise sur le <u>canapé</u>.*   **d** *Je ne l'ai pas <u>goûté</u>.*
   b *Tu vas <u>découper</u> cet article dans le journal?*   **e** *Il ne faut pas <u>sécher</u> les cours.*
   c *C'est <u>dommage</u>.*

Again, the answers are below. That probably took longer, because the dictionary has more than one meaning for each of these words, so you have to use other clues as well (the context, whether it's a verb, a noun, etc). If the word is a verb, you probably need to find the infinitive first – it's not difficult usually, but it does take time. The less you have to use your dictionary, the more time you'll have for studying the French and concentrating on the context.

Use the dictionary:
● to check that you understand the questions and instructions.
● to check what seem to be important words in the text (you rarely need to understand all the words, especially in a longer passage).
● only for words you don't know. It seems obvious, but you can waste a lot of time 'just checking' a word that you really know already.

1 **a** saucer; **b** drinking (water); **c** to punch (a ticket);
   d piece of furniture; **e** alarm clock
2 **a** (in this context) sofa; **b** to cut out; **c** a pity; **d** tasted;
   e to skip (classes)

READING GUIDANCE 2

Coping with some problems

- Handwriting: The handwriting in the exam won't usually be too difficult, and if you have a French pen-friend, you'll have little trouble. However, if the formation of a particular letter is causing you problems, try to find the same letter in a word you already understand. The letter *r* is often hard to read, and the letters *m* and *n* often seem to have a loop too many.

- Passages for reading are often longer and more complex than those for listening. You need to use all the clues in the text to help you break a passage down into manageable bits. Paragraphs, headings, different sizes and types of print (bold, italic, etc) can all help you to identify where there is a change of idea, and highlight key points.

- Once you have read the passage through to get the gist, work from the questions. They will often help you to pinpoint where a particular answer is to be found. Remember, the answers will almost always come in the passage in the same order as the questions, unless they are dealing with the gist of the whole passage.

- There are some structures which you will only meet in the Reading Test, and which you may not be familiar with. A question rarely asks for detailed understanding of them – so as long as you can identify the verb concerned, understanding is not normally a problem.

Strategies for understanding

- Verbs: If you are not sure what verb you are dealing with, first try to identify the ending, and remove it. For example, if you read *ils blanchissent l'argent*, you should recognise *-issent* as a plural ending of an *ir* verb. This will lead you to the infinitive *blanchir*. If you don't immediately realise that this is based on *blanc*, and means 'whiten' (or in this case 'launder') you can look it up in your dictionary.

- Adjectives and nouns: Familarity with irregular feminine or plural endings will often make it easier for you to understand. For example, *nationaux* might seem completely unknown, until you remember that *-aux* is the way in which words ending in *-al* make their plural, so what you are dealing with is the plural of *national*, which isn't too hard to understand.

Similarities with English
● Many French words look almost identical to English words. Although there are dangers (*une journée* is a day, not a journey, and *un car* is a coach, not a car), there aren't too many risks if you use common sense, and check the context. If a word looks like an English word, and the meaning makes sense, it's probably right.
● Very often, words are only similar to English words. There are some common patterns across the two languages, and these will help you to use English/French similarities to best effect.
  – words ending in *-ique* often end in '-ic' in English (*fanatique*);
  – nouns ending in *-té* often end in '-ty' in English (*beauté*);
  – words ending in *-ment* often end in '-ly' in English (*complètement*);
  – present participles ending in *-ant* often match English present participles ending '-ing' (*amusant*);
  – words with a circumflex accent are often like English words which contain an 's' (*pâte* – paste or pasta);
  – verbs which begin *dé-* often begin 'dis-' in English (*découvrir*).

Different types of reading
● Skimming: This is when you know that you are looking for a single, precise piece of information, for example a price. Once you have found it, you can stop. Sometimes it's a little more complicated, for example you may have to look at a number of extracts from letters, and say who has three pets. You have to skim each letter for animals until you find one which contains three.
● Reading for detail: Here, the answer is not quite so easy to pinpoint. Again, you may have a number of extracts from letters, and be asked to identify the person who gets on well with her sister. You can begin by finding references to *sœur*, but then you may have to work a little harder because the verb *s'entendre* might not be used at all – the writer might say that she has the same tastes as her sister, and often goes out with her, leaving you to deduce that they get on well.
● Reading for gist: This will often involve questions in English, and will require you to put together different pieces of information in order to reach a conclusion.

Higher Level skills

- Understanding longer, more complex passages, in which some of the words will not be in the Minimum Core Vocabulary in the syllabus. You should be able to work out (from the context, similarity with English, etc) the meaning of unknown words, using your dictionary if necessary.
- Understanding colloquial expressions and vocabulary (eg *barbant* – boring).
- Reading extracts from fiction. These may include structures such as the past historic or the subjunctive.
- Picking out themes and main points. If you answer this type of question by giving specific details, you may not gain any credit even if they are correct. For example, someone describes a meal in a restaurant as follows:
  Le potage était bon, mais la viande était trop cuite, et les légumes aussi.
  If the question is 'What did he think of the meal?' and you answer that the soup was good or the meat was overcooked, you are not really answering the question. This sort of question is often asked in English.
- Identifying attitudes and opinions. This is not a question of understanding words like *fâché* or *content*, but of working out that when somebody says *J'ai pleuré pendant deux jours*, it means they are upset.
- Choosing from multiple-choice answers in French. First of all, you must make sure that you understand the question, and the gist of the passage. You then need to concentrate on the detail of the passage, until you find one of the suggested answers which fits. You need to understand the suggestions in as much detail as possible, as sometimes they are quite similar, or at least contain some similarities.
- Answering questions in French. There will be at least some questions, probably towards the end of the Higher Level Reading, in which you will have to produce a French phrase or sentence which you can't simply lift from the text. The important thing here is to make sure you know what the question means, and then try to keep your French answer as simple as possible.

Reading 1–4

A Use your dictionary to find out the meanings of the underlined words.

1 Je vais faire le <u>tour</u> du monde.
2 Il a <u>tiré</u> sur les agents de police.
3 Il m'a vu dans la <u>glace</u>. (3)

B Write down the meanings of the underlined words without using your dictionary.

4 Il m'a parlé <u>honnêtement</u>.   5 Le vin était <u>imbuvable</u>.
6 Je n'ai pas aimé le repas – c'était <u>dégoûtant</u>! (3)

C Read these pen-friend adverts, then answer the following questions. You can use the same name more than once.

● Je suis marocaine et je cherche une correspondante américaine. J'adore le cinéma. Je parle le français et l'arabe. **Farah, 12 ans**
● Je peux correspondre en anglais ou en français, avec des garçons ou des filles de mon âge. Mes passions sont le foot, le volley et le ski. J'adore aussi la photographie. **Baptiste ,15 ans**
● J'aime la télé et la lecture. Je voudrais correspondre en français avec des jeunes de tous pays. **Aurore, 14 ans**
● Je cherche un(e) jeune qui partage mes goûts – les sports nautiques et la musique rap. J'adore les voyages. Je peux correspondre en français, en anglais ou en arabe. **Rafik, 13 ans**

7 Qui connaît bien trois langues?
8 Qui veut correspondre avec une fille?
9 Qui est très sportif?   11 Qui ne parle qu'une langue?
10 Qui aime lire?   12 Qui aime voyager? (6)

D Choose a word from the list to complete each blank.

Une __13__ de handball se __14__ entre deux équipes de __15__ joueurs. C'est un peu __16__ le foot à cinq, mais on joue uniquement avec les __17__ . Un __18__ peut __19__ le ballon dans le but, passer à un __20__ , ou dribbler (comme au basket).

A pieds   **B** sept   **C** adversaire   **D** partie   **E** lancer
F joueur   **G** partenaire   **H** joue   **I** mains   **J** comme (8)

A

1 tour 'Tower' doesn't make sense here, and in any case, it's feminine in French.
2 fired (or shot at) The verb *tirer* has a number of other meanings:
   a) to pull – so you might find *Tirez* on a door.
   b) to draw – but only with curtains, not a picture!
3 mirror 'He saw me in the ice-cream' doesn't make much sense, and 'He saw me in the ice' isn't much better. (3)

B If you use some of the strategies on the Guidance Cards, and are aware of similarities between French and English, it can save you a lot of time with the dictionary.

4 honestly The circumflex accent often indicates a missing 's'.
5 undrinkable Use of *im-* or *in-* before a word often means 'un-', and *-able* is the same as the English, so all you then need to do is to see the link between *buv* and the verb *boire* (*buvons*).
6 disgusting Again, *dé-* often means 'dis-', and *-ant* often means '-ing'. (3)

C

7 Rafik He can write in French, English or Arabic.
8 Farah She specifies *une correspondante*.
9 Baptiste He mentions three sports.
10 Aurore Check *lire* and *lecture* in your dictionary.
11 Aurore She is only willing to write in French.
12 Rafik The link is between the verb *voyager* and the noun *voyages*. (6)

D

13 D **14** H **15** B **16** J **17** I **18** F **19** E **20** G (8)
If you look for grammatical links, you can sometimes do some of this type of exercise even if you're not sure of the meaning of the word. The answer to 14 must be the third person singular of a verb, and *joue* is the only possibility, (even if it's not usually reflexive). In 19, only an infinitive can follow *peut* – again, there is only one possibility.

Reading 1–4

A *Vrai, faux ou on ne sait pas?* Read the advert, then indicate if the statements are true (V) false (F) or not told (?).

1 Il y a une télévision dans toutes les chambres.
2 Il y a un parking à l'hôtel.
3 L'hôtel est près de la gare. (3)

> *Hotel Croix D'or*
> 27 chambres, toutes avec WC, dont:
> 15 avec douche 6 avec salle de bains
> Dans la plupart de nos chambres,
> télévision couleurs et téléphone.
> Parking sur la place principale.

B Match the halves of these extracts from an invitation.

4 Salut Louise! Veux-tu ...
5 Ça commence ...
6 Apporte ...

A ... vers huit heures trente.
B ... vraiment super.
C ... quelque chose à boire.
D ... aller à une boum? (3)

C Read what these people have to say about their jobs, then say who would make each statement below.

Maxime Tous les samedis et dimanches je travaille dans la cuisine d'un restaurant. Je fais la vaisselle, et j'aide le chef. C'est très dur, mais je gagne assez pour m'acheter des vêtements.

Floriane Avec l'argent que me donnent mes parents, je n'ai pas besoin de travailler, mais je préfère gagner mon propre argent – comme ça je peux le dépenser comme je veux – donc je travaille dans un magasin.

Alexandre Moi, je travaille dans une épicerie, mais ce n'est pas très bien payé, alors je cherche un autre petit job, peut-être dans un hôtel, car l'année prochaine je veux acheter une moto.

Noémie Je fais du baby-sitting. Je ne gagne pas beaucoup, mais mes parents m'achètent mes vêtements, et je ne sors pas souvent, alors ça va.

7 Travailler me donne un peu d'indépendance.
8 Je voudrais changer d'emploi.
9 Je n'ai pas besoin de beaucoup d'argent.
10 Je m'intéresse à la mode – et c'est cher!
11 Le problème, c'est que je ne peux pas sortir le week-end.
12 Je travaille pour faire des économies. (6)

D **Read the passage, then answer the questions in English.**

Pourquoi parle-t-on de plus en plus de la violence au lycée?

Lycéens raquettés, profs agressés, établissements saccagés: en 1998 la violence à l'école a fait régulièrement la une des médias.

Un collégien tué par balle à Montereau, des enseignants agressés dans un lycée professionnel de Lyon, des violences dans un collège de Toulouse, des tentatives d'incendie dans un collège à Poitiers, l'assassinat d'un collégien pour une paire de gants à Valence ...

Selon les derniers chiffres de la direction centrale de la sécurité publique, les coups et blessures à l'encontre d'élèves ou de personnel de l'Education nationale ont augmenté de plus de 19% entre 1996 et 1997. Le racket a doublé en cinq ans.

Ces chiffres indiquent une réelle augmentation de la violence, mais aussi une meilleure prise en compte du phénomène par la police et les chefs d'établissements. Aujourd'hui, élèves et professeurs parlent plus et, parfois, font grève pour exprimer ainsi leur ras-le-bol.

13 What is the article about? (3)

14 What sort of educational establishments are mainly affected? (1)

15 What frequently happened in 1998? (2)

16 How are teachers and pupils reacting to the problem? (2)

ANSWERS & TUTORIALS   SCORE

A

| 1 F | 2 F | 3 ? | (3) |

B

| 4 D | 5 A | 6 C | (3) |

C

| 7 Floriane | 8 Alexandre | 9 Noémie |
| 10 Maxime | 11 Maxime | 12 Alexandre | (6) |

D

13 Increasing (1) violence (1) in schools (1)

14 Secondary OR all OR *collèges* and *lycées* (1)

15 Violence in schools in the news (1) on the front page (1)

16 Talking about it (1); going on strike (1)

As in speaking, you have one great advantage in writing: there is always some choice of content, and therefore of language, in the test. Some boards actually give you a choice of question. If this is the case for you, make sure you choose wisely. Don't spend too long on the choice, but look at the topics, and ask yourself which one you feel happiest with. Do you know a lot of the vocabulary? Do you know some ready-made phrases which would fit? Are there many words which you will have to use (for example in a narrative based on pictures) that you'll need to look up? Even if the paper set by your board does not give you any choice of question, you can still to some extent choose what to say.

Understanding the question

Make sure that you are familiar with the layout of the paper. The general pattern will remain the same from year to year, and the early questions in particular will always ask for similar things. However, in the later questions, and at Higher Level, you must make sure that you understand what you have to do, using your dictionary if necessary.

Deciding what you want to write

- Don't start by working out in detail in English what you want to say, and then translating it into French. You will always end up trying to say things you have never learnt, which means you may get the structures wrong and will have to look up lots of words.
- Don't be in too much of a rush to get started. Many candidates aim to finish in time to make a 'fair copy' of what they have written. This is usually a bad idea, as you don't really have time. You often end up simply copying the mistakes you made in the first draft, and adding a few new ones as you rush to get finished.
- Do start by making a plan. This needn't take long, but it will help you to know where you're going. If the question gives you a series of tasks to do, make a note – at this stage in English if you like – of what each task is, and of some useful words and phrases in French. If your task is to reply to a French prompt, such as a letter which asks a number of questions, jot down in English the questions which are asked, and then list some useful French words and phrases.

Producing accurate work

Unfortunately, there is no easy answer to this. However, there is one thing you can do to minimise mistakes, and that is to check your work:

● Make sure that verbs agree with their subject. Common errors are to put a singular ending after *ils* or *elles* (often putting *-e* instead of *-ent*, or *-ait* instead of *-aient*). If you're in a hurry, you can at least check that after *tu* your verb ends in *-s*, and that after *il*//*elle*/someone's name the verb does **not** end in *-s*.

● Make sure that all your perfect tense verbs have the correct part of *avoir* or *être* as well as the past participle. The commonest verb error of all is to write, for example, *je parlé* instead of *j'ai parlé*.

● Check that if you've used an adjective with a feminine or plural noun, you've made the adjective feminine or plural too.

Completing all the tasks

If you forget to do one of the tasks you will certainly lose marks for content, and probably other marks too. Either on the question paper, or on your plan, tick each task as you do it.

Using the dictionary

Using the dictionary for the Writing Test is a different skill from using it in the Reading Test. To begin with, you are using the other half of the dictionary! You should keep in mind the following points:

● Only use the dictionary when you need to – as little as possible.

● Words with different meanings are more of a problem when you are using the English/French section of the dictionary. In English, you'll probably know instinctively whether you've got the right word, but how do you know in French? For example, if you want to say 'I hope I'll pass the exam', and you're not sure of the French for 'pass', you look it up, and you'll find (at least) the following French words: *le col*; *une passe*; *une carte*; *passer*; *être reçu*. How do you choose? Hopefully, you will realise that what you need is a verb, which limits you to the last two choices. To decide, you need to check any examples given, which should lead you to choose the last verb and to write *J'espère que je serai reçu(e) à l'examen*.

WRITING GUIDANCE 3

Higher Level tasks

In addition to the simple messages required at Foundation, you might be asked to write:

- Letters: These may be personal letters (to a penfriend, for example) or more formal letters (booking a room at a hotel, or applying for a job). It is most important to begin and end your letter correctly:
  – A business letter will usually begin simply *Monsieur* or *Madame*; a letter to a friend should begin *Cher* or *Chère* plus the first name.
  – You can end an informal letter with *Amitiés* or *Grosses bises* (very informal, only to someone you know well!), while the most straightforward way of ending a business letter is probably *Veuillez agréer, monsieur/madame, l'expression de mes sentiments distingués*.
  The tasks set for a letter will usually require you to ask questions. In an informal letter, it is fine to use the colloquial question form *Tu aimes la musique pop?*, but you must remember the question mark.

- Articles: The content of these may not be very different from a letter, but they are more likely to stick to one subject, and will possibly be in the third person (*il* or *elle*) rather than the first person. It is more important in an article to make sure that you arrange what you write in a logical way, so that links between ideas are clear.

- Accounts: These are always in the past. You may have to write about a recent exchange visit, or what you did on work experience, or you may have to base your account on a series of pictures – check what sort of questions your own examining group uses. In an account based on pictures, you do **not** have to write about every detail of every picture, but you should say at least something about each picture. It is often useful to assume that you will write about the same amount about each picture.

Some examining groups specify on the question paper how much you are expected to write, while others give suggested lengths in the syllabus. As a rough guide, you probably need to write about 90 words for the first question on the Higher paper (which is also the last question on the Foundation paper), and about 120 words for the second question. The most important thing is to complete all the tasks.

Higher Level skills

In order to get a Grade C or higher, you must do the following:

- Refer to past, present and future events. If the question you are answering has specified tasks, you will not be able to complete all the tasks without doing this. In a letter it is easy to refer to all three:

  J'espère que tu vas bien. (present)

  J'ai fini mes examens. (past)

  Cet été je vais (or *je vais aller* or *j'irai*) *aux Etats-Unis.* (future)

  In an account – which is basically in the past – you may need to consciously try to put in a future. If it is about a French exchange, you might say at the end: *L'année prochaine ma correspondante viendra chez moi en Angleterre.*

- Express personal opinions. This is not normally a problem, since it was one of the first things you learned to do in French.

There are a number of things you need to do to go beyond Grade C:

- Write longer sentences. This need not be difficult, but it does mean using linking words (*mais, puis, alors, donc*) appropriately.

- Use *qui* and *que*. Even used quite simply, they add an extra dimension to your language, and create longer sentences:

  J'ai une sœur qui s'appelle Louise.

  Tu aimes les fleurs que j'ai achetées?

- Express more complicated ideas and opinions. Rather than just *j'aime*, etc, use expressions like:

  à mon avis (in my opinion)

  je pense que (I think that)

  ce n'est pas juste (it's not fair)

- Include more than the minimum detail. Add adjectives or adverbs to expand on the bare facts.

- Give reasons or explanations:

  J'aime aller en France car il fait beau.

  Ce soir je ne peux pas, car j'ai des devoirs à faire.

- Use as wide a variety of language as you can. Avoid too much repetition – especially lists with *il y a* – and use a range of tenses:

  Ma mère était très contente du cadeau.

  Si j'avais assez d'argent, j'achèterais une grosse voiture.

Writing 1–4

A **Answer these questions in French:**

1 Tu as un animal à la maison?

2 Tu aimes le sport?

3 Qu'est-ce qu tu aimes regarder à la télé?

4 Que fais-tu le soir?

(4)

Remember that when you are answering questions in a letter, your answers need to stand alone – you can't assume that your penfriend still has a copy of the questions he or she asked!

B **Say in French:**

5 I have worked in a restaurant before. (2)
6 I'm going to see my grandmother. (2)
7 On Saturdays I go into town. (2)
8 I'd like to be a vet. (2)

C **Complete the following tasks:**

9 Say what you did last weekend. (2)
10 Say what you intend to do when you leave school. (2)
11 Describe what you usually do during the summer holidays. (2)
12 Explain why you like/dislike school. (2)

Use at least two verbs for each task, and add an extra detail to each sentence or phrase. As in **A**, make sure your sentences stand alone.

A

1 J'ai un chien et un poisson. You need to give both details to score the mark.

2 J'aime le tennis et le cyclisme. Again, you need both details.

3 J'aime (regarder) les films à la télé. It doesn't make much difference whether you use *regarder* or not, but *à la télé* **must** be there to get the right message across.

4 Le soir je fais mes devoirs. There are sometimes different ways of interpreting visuals. As long as yours is sensible, it will get the credit: *Je travaille dans ma chambre* would be equally good here. (4)

B

5 J'ai déjà travaillé dans un restaurant. (2) You need to use *déjà* here, not *avant*.

6 Je vais voir ma grand-mère. (2) Don't forget this very easy way of referring to future events.

7 Le samedi je vais en ville. (2) Remember that to express something that you always/frequently do on the same day of the week, you use *le* + the day.

8 Je voudrais devenir vétérinaire. (2) This is another useful way of referring to what is going to happen.

C The extra details are underlined. Give yourself one mark if you get two verbs (in 9 they must be past, in 10 future, in 11 and 12 present), and another mark if you get two extra details. Make sure that you check the accuracy of what you have written before you give yourself the marks!

9 Le week-end dernier je suis allé(e) au cinéma <u>avec mes amis</u>. Nous avons vu un film <u>d'amour</u>. (2)

10 Après le lycée, j'irai à l'université <u>pour étudier les sciences</u>, car je voudrais être professeur <u>de physique</u>. (2)

11 Pendant les grandes vacances, je vais au bord de la mer <u>avec mes copains</u>. Nous jouons sur la plage <u>s'il fait beau</u>. (2)

12 Je n'aime pas le collège parce que j'ai trop de devoirs à faire <u>chaque soir</u>, et je déteste les profs, <u>surtout le prof de maths</u>. (2)

You can see from the examples above that the extra details can vary from quite complex phrases including verbs, to just a couple of words.

Writing 1–4

Exam-style questions

A Foundation/Higher

Vous avez reçu cette lettre de ta nouvelle corespondante, Gabrielle.
Lisez sa lettre, puis écrivez une réponse en français.
Répondez à toutes les questions. Ecrivez 100 mots. (10)

> Salut!
> Je suis ta nouvelle correspondante.
> Je m'appelle Gabrielle. J'ai seize ans. Nous
> sommes quatre personnes dans ma famille. Et toi? Il y
> a combien de personnes dans ta famille? Tu as
> combien de frères et sœurs? (1)
> Je vais au collège à Dieppe. J'adore le collège. Il est
> comment, ton collège? Quelles matières aimes-tu? (2)
> Pendant les vacances d'été, nous sommes allés en
> Italie. Qu'est-ce que tu as fait pendant les grandes
> vacances? (3)
> Je suis très sportive. Tu aimes le sport, toi? Quels
> sont tes passe-temps préférés? (4)
> Qu'est-ce que tu vas faire après l'école? (5) Moi, je
> vais devenir infirmière, comme ma mère.
> Amitiés
> Gabrielle

(The numbers in the letter refer you to the Answers & Tutorial.)

B Higher

Vous cherchez un emploi en France. Ecrivez une lettre en français
au directeur d'une colonie de vacances.

6 – Dites pourquoi vous voulez travailler avec des enfants.
7 – Décrivez votre personnalité. (Donnez trois détails.)
8 – Décrivez deux emplois que vous avez déjà eus.
9 – Dites jusqu'à quand vous pourrez travailler, et pourquoi.
10 – Dites pourquoi vous voulez travailler en France. (10)

A To get full credit, you need to give two details for each answer.

1 Any two of the following (1 mark each). Obviously the precise details – eg number of people in family – are variable.
Il y a quatre personnes dans ma famille.   J'ai deux sœurs.
J'ai un frère.   Je n'ai pas de sœurs/frères. OR Je suis fille/fils unique.

2 Mon collège est grand/petit. OR Il y a sept cents élèves (etc).
(1) J'aime l'histoire et la géographie (etc). (1) There must be **two** subjects, though it would probably be OK to put one you like and one you dislike.

3 (Pendant les grandes vacances) je suis allé(e) en France avec mes parents. (1) Nous avons fait du camping. (1) These **must** be in the past. If you say where you went and what you did, you will use two different verbs.

4 (Oui) j'adore le sport. (1) It's a good idea to avoid the verb in the question if you can, but it isn't always possible.
J'aime aussi aller au cinéma et écouter de la musique. (1) Again, the question requires two pastimes.

5 Moi, je ne veux pas être professeur, comme mon père. (1) It's often possible to reply using a negative, to add a little variety.
Je voudrais travailler dans un bureau. (1) To change from *être* or *devenir*, you can always say **where** you want to work.

B You must give more than a minimum response to score highly.

6 Je veux travailler avec les enfants <u>parce que j'ai beaucoup de petits cousins et cousines</u>, (1) et <u>je m'occupe souvent d'eux</u>. (1) One mark for a reason, and one for an extra detail.

7 Je suis assez timide, mais je m'entends bien avec les gens, et je suis consciencieux(se). (2) Only one mark for two details, zero for only one detail. One mark only if each detail was an adjective.

8 J'ai travaillé dans un hôtel, et j'ai fait la vaisselle dans un café. (2) Only one mark if only one verb (or the same verb twice).

9 Je peux travailler jusqu'à la fin d'août, car les cours recommencent le deux septembre. (2) One mark for the first part, and one for the reason.

10 Je veux travailler en France pour améliorer mon français, et parce que j'aime la cuisine française. (2) Only one mark if only one verb (or the same verb twice).

SCORE CARD (1)

Topic	*Check yourself card*	Points out of 20
L'école	1	
A la maison/les média	2	
La santé, la forme et la nourriture	3	
Moi, ma famille et mes amis	4	
Le temps libre, les loisirs, les vacances et les fêtes	5	
Rapports personnels, activités sociales et rendez-vous	6	
La ville, les régions, le temps	7	
Les courses, les services publics	8	
La route, les voyages et les transports	9	
L'enseignement supérieur, la formation et l'emploi	10	
La publicité, les communications et les langues au travail	11	
La vie à l'étranger, le tourisme, les coutûmes et le logement	12	
Le monde	13	
Nouns, articles, adverbs	14	
Adjectives, adverbs	15	
Pronouns	16	
Demonstratives, indefinites, intensifiers	17	
Numbers, quantities, dates, time	18	
Prepositions, conjunctions, interrogatives	19	
Verbs – present tense	20	
Verbs – past tenses	21	
Verbs – future tenses	22	
Verbs – general	23	
Listening 1–4	24	
Speaking I 1–4	25	
Speaking II 1–4	26	
Reading I 1–4	27	
Reading II 1–4	28	
Writing I 1–4	29	
Writing II 1–4	30	

SCORE CARD (2)

Mark your points for each card on the grid and then
read across for your grade.

GCSE Grade

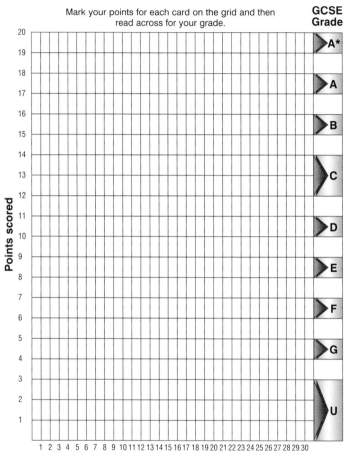

Check yourself card